ONE-DISH
DINNERS

Autumn Beef Stew, page 88

ONE-DISH
DINNERS

RODALE®

Cover photograph: Mitch Mandel
Cover recipe: Jambalaya on-the-Bayou
            Courtesy of Zatarain's, page 124
Food Stylist: Diane Vezza
Illustrations: Judy Newhouse

Editorial Produced by:
BETH ALLEN ASSOCIATES, INC.

President/Owner: Beth Allen
Art Production Director: Laura Smyth (smythtype)
Culinary Consultant/Food Editor: Deborah Mintcheff
Recipe Editor: Jackie Mills
Public Relations Consultants: Stephanie Avidon, Melissa Moritz
Nutritionist: Michele C. Fisher, Ph.D., R.D.

Library of Congress Cataloging-in-Publication Data

One-dish dinners.
        p.   cm.
    Includes index.
    ISBN-13 978–1–59486–142–0 hardcover
    ISBN-10 1–59486–142–0 hardcover
    1. Casserole cookery.
TX693.O447   2005
641.8'21—dc22   2004021315

2   4   6   8   10   9   7   5   3   hardcover

RODALE

WE **INSPIRE** AND **ENABLE** PEOPLE TO IMPROVE
THEIR LIVES AND THE WORLD AROUND THEM

FOR **MORE** OF OUR **PRODUCTS**

WWW.RODALESTORE.COM
(800) 848-4735

CONTENTS

INTRODUCTION

Much more than your mother's covered dish!

Remember your mom's chicken-noodle casserole? Chock full of broad egg noodles, fresh mushrooms, and chunky pieces of chicken left over from Sunday's bird—all covered with a rich, creamy sauce? One delicious bite, and you knew everything was "loving and good" . . . it was comfort food at its best! That same great flavor and simple goodness, all from one dish—that's what this book is all about.

One-Dish Dinners is unique. It's not just casseroles, though we've included a few favorites. It's any recipe where all of the main cooking happens in one pot or one dish. In some recipes, we help you speed it all up by cooking something in a second pot or dish, such as boiling noodles or steaming rice in a pot or cooking carrots in the microwave. And since we know that some days you probably don't have time for any cooking at all, we've even added some suppers-in-a-salad or meals-in-a-sandwich that can be served as one dish.

Unlike covered dishes of long ago, the 100 recipes in this book are all fast to fix! Those carrying the *SuperQuick* label even go from pantry to table in 30 minutes or less. How about Creamy Skillet Turkey (page 40) for supper tonight? Serve it over buttered noodles and it tastes just like those old-fashioned casseroles—but the best part is that it's ready to eat in a third of the time. Or turn frozen stir-fry vegetables into Sweet & Sour Pork (page 34) and serve it up over instant steamed rice in just 20 minutes. And don't forget that overstuffed sandwich that's supper-on-one-plate, too, such as Speedy Meatball Sandwiches (page 68), made fast as a flash from fully cooked meatballs from your grocer's freezer.

What's a one-dish cookbook without a chili or a stew? Naturally they're here, too, often cooked in less time than you ever thought possible, thanks to convenience mixes and precooked ingredients from the freezer. Pull out your cooking pot and try our Fast & Easy Beef Chili Pot (page 90) or our Shrimp Creole Stew (page 91), with all of those flavors from down on the bayou. Quickly layer up your baking dish with our No-Fuss Beef Lasagna (page 98). It goes together in minutes—you don't even have to cook the noodles first. And when it comes to having friends over for dinner on the weekends, our Quick Cook one-dish dinners are the answer. There's a pot roast that takes just minutes to put into the pan, thanks to frozen ready-to-eat vegetables, and a roast chicken that roasts inside a bag, which means easy cleanup.

But *One-Dish Dinners* is filled with much more than recipes. The very next page introduces our new take on "Easy Dinner in a Dish." In this chapter, you'll find five fabulous new techniques for one-dish suppers, such as cooking a little to get a head start on a different dish for tomorrow and layering different flavors in the pot to make the best-tasting dinners ever. Take a minute to learn what to stock your pantry with to help keep one-dish dinners on the fast track. Then pick one of our super-easy "5 Fast One-Skillet Suppers" to make tonight. Check out the latest pots that go beautifully from stove to table, cutting down on dishwashing later.

But all of this is just for starters. The 100 flavor-packed one-dish dinners collected here are a true team effort. They come from professional test kitchens of well-known food manufacturers and talented cooking pros. We all have one goal in mind: to bring you great one-dish dinners, all kitchen-tested to ensure perfect results every time. Some recipes come with *On the Menu* ideas for fast-to-serve side dishes, while others have *Microwave in Minutes* suggestions on how to jump-start the cooking to cut the baking time later.

Look for helpful new *Cooking Basics* throughout the pages, including "Pouch Cooking—Easy as A, B, C!," and *Cook to Cook* tips from folks on how to adapt that favorite recipe to a slow cooker. And look inside the *Food Facts* boxes to discover tidbits such as how tetrazzini got its name (the answer's on page 26).

Start right now enjoying the many quick-cooking tips and techniques for making *One-Dish Dinners* now. Remember that there are many other books in The Quick Cook series, too. Each book will become a great kitchen helper. They all focus on just what you need in today's cookbooks— quick-cooking recipes, beautiful photographs, tried-and-true techniques, and helpful tips.

Start reading, start cooking, and start discovering how easy it is to serve those fabulous one-dish comfort foods—faster, fresher, and quicker than ever before.

Creamy Tuna Noodle Casserole, page 21

Easy Dinner in a Dish

This is it: the fastest, simplest, most foolproof way to serve up dinner—all in the same dish it was cooked in. Turn the page and choose a recipe, then grab a few ingredients, your favorite skillet, and a large spoon. You'll be at the dinner table in no time at all. Cook a little extra and you'll have a head start the next day on a whole new dish. The best part: You don't need much time to create these recipes. Many use convenience foods, such as ready-to-eat rice in a pouch, frozen vegetables, fresh refrigerated pastas, cooked shrimp, ready-to-eat microwaveable rice, and sauce in a jar. And each finished dish is layered with flavor in each delicious bite. Stir up a fast one-dish dinner tonight!

Curried Chicken & 'Tater Stew, page 111

Cheese Steak Pizza, page 27

Honey Couscous Salad, page 63

THE NEW ONE-DISH

Everything old is new again—sort of. Grandma's casseroles and covered one-dish meals are still around and more popular than ever. Today we call it comfort food, and it still tastes as great and homemade as ever—but were she around today, she might be surprised to see a few of the changes.

• New super-speedy ingredients. Grandma never had it so easy! Many of our Quick Cook recipes have extra shortcuts built in, such as no-cook lasagna noodles and fresh, fast-cooking linguine. Others use convenience foods, such as ready-to-eat meatballs or sauce mixes. For more options, see "One-Pot Pantry" on page 15.

• Finer ingredients. Look at the classic chicken-noodle casserole: It can now use free-range chicken (freshly cooked, of course), exotic mushrooms, and unusual shaped pastas, such as ripple-edged noodles called *mafalda*.

• Goodness in a jar. There's a lot of extra flavor in jars these days: pesto, roasted peppers, and caramelized red onions that add a lovely sweetness to savory dishes.

IT'S ALL IN THE DISH

Gone are the days when a casserole or covered dish was made of only breakable, heat-resistant glass. There are so many more wonderful options today:

• Stoneware and ceramic bakeware go from the freezer to the microwave, oven, and dishwasher. They're mass-produced, easy on the pocketbook, and look great on the table.

• Handmade, one-of-a-kind pottery bakers are the highest on looks, often crafted by artisans. They're made to go into the oven but can crack if exposed to long intense heat. They're fine in the freezer or microwave, but should be hand-washed (most are not dishwasher safe).

• Enameled bakeware (cast iron or stainless steel) has a great advantage for one-dish cooking: It can go safely to the stove top for browning, then into the oven for more cooking. It's safe in the freezer but not in the microwave. Handle with care, as the colorful "glass" enamel can chip.

• Copper au gratin are ideal for one-dish dinners, which begin on the top of the range then go into the oven or under the broiler—but not into the microwave. Be sure to buy ones that are lined with stainless steel (not tin).

Cooking Basics

5 FAST ONE-SKILLET SUPPERS

Skillet cooking is one of the fastest types of cooking there is. And that's why it's such an important part of many Quick Cook recipes. Grab your skillet, pull together a few ingredients, and start cooking with these super-speedy recipes. Each one turns into supper in just 30 minutes or less.

SHRIMP CREOLE Cook 1 packet of microwaveable ready-to-heat rice according to the package directions. Meanwhile, sauté 1 chopped medium onion, 1 slivered large green bell pepper, and 2 minced garlic cloves in 2 tablespoons oil until soft. Stir in one 14½-ounce can stewed tomatoes (preferably a Cajun recipe) and heat until bubbly. Add 1¼ pounds deveined, shelled large shrimp and stir-fry for 3 minutes, or until shrimp are pink. Stir the cooked rice into the shrimp mixture and remove from the heat. Cover and let stand for 5 minutes so the flavors can blend. Pass the hot pepper sauce, please!

SAUSAGE ITALIEN Brown 1 pound Italian sausage, 1 medium chopped onion, 1 chopped large red bell pepper, and 1 minced garlic clove in 1 tablespoon oil until the sausage is no longer pink and the vegetables are soft. Stir in one 26-ounce jar marinara pasta sauce and heat until bubbly. Toss in 3 cups cooked rotini and remove from the heat. Cover and let stand for 5 minutes so the flavors can blend. Sprinkle with slivered basil.

FILET PARISIENNE Cut a 1-pound rib-eye steak into thin strips. Sauté 4 ounces sliced mushrooms, ¾ cup chopped scallions, and 1 minced garlic clove in 2 tablespoons of butter until tender. Push the vegetables to one side of the skillet and sauté the beef strips in the center of the skillet, just to your liking. Stir in 1 cup sour cream until blended, then gently fold in 3 cups cooked, drained egg noodles (the fresh refrigerated ones cook the fastest). Remove from the heat, cover, and let stand for 5 minutes so the flavors can blend.

CHICKEN RICE ORIENTAL Sauté a 1 pound boneless, skinless chicken breast strips with 1 chopped medium onion and 1 minced garlic clove until the chicken juices run clear. Meanwhile, cook 1 packet of microwaveable ready-to-heat long-grain rice according to the package directions. Stir the rice into the chicken mixture, along with 2 tablespoons soy sauce. Remove from the heat, cover, and let stand for 5 minutes so the flavors can blend.

SAUCY SALSA BEEF Cook 1 pound lean ground beef in 1 tablespoon oil along with 1 chopped medium onion and one 1¼-ounce packet taco seasoning mix until the beef loses its pink color. Stir in 1 cup salsa. Sprinkle with 1 cup shredded pepper Jack cheese (do not stir in). Remove from the heat, cover, and let stand for 5 minutes, or until the cheese melts. Sprinkle with crumbled taco chips. Serve over hot cooked rice, if you like.

Cajun Pork Paella, page 114

These go elegantly to the table and can go into the freezer, but they often do not have covers. Hand-wash, please!

• Anodized aluminum, with its smoky gray looks, is fine on the stovetop, oven, and freezer, but not in the microwave. Its coated interior keeps it from reacting to acidic ingredients (which regular aluminum does).

• Skillets should have heat-safe handles that go under the broiler and into the oven.

Most one-dish recipes—especially casseroles—often specify the volume a dish should hold, not its exact dimensions size. Here's a quick guide to knowing if the dish you want to use is the right size:

2-quart casserole = 8-inch square baking dish
2-quart casserole = 11 × 7-inch baking dish
2½-quart casserole = 9-inch square baking dish
3-quart casserole = 13 × 9-inch baking dish

ONE DISH TODAY, A DIFFERENT ONE TOMORROW

Many recipes in this book make more than can be eaten at one meal. But what's left over can become the basis for a brand-new dish. Here are a few to try:

POT ROAST Shred the meat that's left from the pot roast and add it to the pan gravy. Add two 14½-ounce cans stewed tomatoes (preferably Italian style) and heat until bubbly. Toss in some slivered fresh basil. Serve over hot pasta. Or use leftover pot roast for making fajitas, enchiladas, or tacos.

CHILI Turn leftover chili into Chili Beans and Rice: Add ½ to 1 cup canned kidney beans (depending on the amount already in the chili) and 1 cup salsa. Simmer until bubbly. Spoon over steamed white rice. Top with chopped avocado, sliced green onions, shredded Cheddar, and sliced black olives. Pass the salsa. Or turn the leftover chili into a taco salad: Line a plate with taco chips, cover with shredded iceberg lettuce, and top with hot chili. Sprinkle with sliced green onions and shredded Monterey Jack, then garnish with a dollop of sour cream.

STEW Turn leftovers into a potpie: Begin with a 9-inch pie plate and a 15-ounce package of refrigerated pie crusts or enough homemade pastry for a double-crust pie. Line the pie plate with crust and fill with the stew. Top with the second crust and flute the edges. Cut slits in several places and bake at 425°F for 25 minutes, or until golden brown and bubbly.

Mediterranean Steak Sandwiches, page 74

*Lemon Dill Salmon
with Red Potatoes, page 80*

Beef & Noodles Stroganoff, page 99

LAYERING IN THE FLAVORS

The success of your one-dish dinner depends upon how good it tastes. Layering in the flavors is the secret.

• When browning ingredients, be sure to scrape up the crispy pieces on the bottom of the skillet or pot—and keep them in the dish.

• Season often as you add ingredients to the pot. Slowly build up the flavors and taste as you go—don't wait to season at the end.

• If cooking pasta or rice that will be added to the pot, season its cooking water.

• As a general rule, simmer, don't boil!

• When adding fresh herbs to the pot, save a little to garnish the pot. This adds an extra layer of fresh flavor and enticing fragrance on top, right before serving.

• When the dish is done, transfer to a cooling rack and let it stand for 5 minutes. This lets the many flavor layers blend and permeate even more.

• Remember, flavors intensify as soups, stews, and casseroles chill in the refrigerator. This means, they taste better the next day. If the recipe can be made ahead, do it. You'll be glad you did!

• Garnish with extra flavor! Crumbled bacon adds a "smoke-house touch" to a chowder. A cooling dollop of sour cream showered with minced scallions adds an authentic touch to a Mexican dish. Freshly grated Parmesan and fresh basil are great toppers for an Italian recipe. Such garnishes add yet another layer of flavor to the dish.

DINNER IN A DISH—TO GO!

When planning to carry a one-dish dinner to a friend's home, a large gathering, or a picnic, keep it steaming hot (or icy cold) and keep it safe! Here are a few tips:

• Reach for your picnic cooler—it's not just for keeping foods cold. These coolers are insulated, so they'll hold in the "hot" as well.

Cooking Basics

ONE-POT PANTRY

Want to turn those favorite hand-me-down one-dish recipes into something new? First, stock up with plenty of different pastas, flavored sauces, and various cheeses. Here are a few (both new and overlooked) that we've found to get you started:

• Cheese. Have fun with the cheese you put in a dish. If your recipe calls for a cheese sauce made with Cheddar, try one or two different cheeses: blue cheese (try the mildest flavored one, dolce Gorgonzola), Brie (the French semisoft classic), Cambozola (a German cheese that's a cross between Gorgonzola and Brie), Gruyère, or Monterey Jack (it comes peppered, too, with a bite).

• Macaroni. Try new pasta shapes that really hold on to the sauce when making familiar favorites like mac 'n' cheese: *cappelletti* ("little hats"), *cavatappi* (corkscrews), *cavatelli* (small shells with rippled edges), *ditali* (short tubes of macaroni), or *ruote de carro* (small "cartwheels").

• Noodles and pastas. When tossing noodles and pastas into long-cooking recipes, use dried. For short-cooking one-dish dinners,

such as our recipes cooked fast in a skillet, look for fresh pastas in the refrigerated case at your grocer or in gourmet markets. Have fun trying new shapes. For instance, instead of using the familiar thin egg noodles, try the broad ones (they give more sauce in every bite). Also consider: *farfalle* ("butterflies"), *mafalda* (broad, ripple-edges noodles resembling mini-lasagna noodles), *rotelle* (short spirals), *radiatore* ("little radiators").

• Pasta sauce, beyond marinara. There are plenty of tomato-based pasta sauces in cans and jars. Look for these: *arrabbiata* ("angry"; very spicy with chiles and pancetta), four cheese, spiced up tomato, mini meatball, mushroom marinara, primavera, ricotta and Parmesan, roasted garlic and herb, sun-dried tomato, Vidalia onion, and vodka sauce.

• Rice 'n' spice. The news in rice is both the easy, fast packet-packaging and the new varieties and spices. Ready-to-eat rice comes in packets that go straight into the microwave and "cook" in just 90 seconds. Other rice packets cook the normal way in 10 minutes, in a saucepan or in the microwave. Rice comes in different varieties,

such as Arborio, basmati, and jasmine. They are often Spanish-, lemon-and-herb-, or chicken-flavored. To replace rice with different grains in one-dish recipes consider: bulghur wheat (used in the Middle Eastern dish of tabbouleh), orzo (Italian for "barley"), and couscous (granular semolina used in North African cuisine). Cook them according to the package directions before substituting them for the cooked rice in a recipe.

• Toppers and garnishes. Once upon a time, casseroles, soup, stews, and one-dish dinners were topped with bread crumbs, parsley, or cheese. Consider the variety that now exists. Pesto is a purée of fresh basil leaves, pine nuts, the best extra virgin olive oil, Parmesan, and garlic. Make it fresh or buy it ready made. Spoon over a hearty tomato-based soup or a hot Italian pasta skillet. Croutons make perfect one-dish toppers. Make them fresh or buy them; toss them whole or crush them first. Look for croutons flavored with pepper, herbs, Parmesan, or garlic. Or for a different topping, sliver and "frizzle" some onions by frying them until golden and crispy.

Cheesy Grits, page 24

Shrimp Gumbo, page 93

No-Fuss Beef Lasagna, page 98

• Turn a turkey roaster into a toting basket. First, line it with clean kitchen towels. Put in the covered dish and tuck more towels around it, insulating the dish and keeping it steady.

• Keep the dish covered during its journey, even if it didn't cook covered. If you don't have a cover, use heavy-duty aluminum foil.

Take a few moments to browse through *One-Dish Dinner* recipes and plan which ones to try right away. Here are some of our favorites:

Chicken & Rice Casserole   (page 20)

Beefy Vegetable Skillet   (page 36)

Linguini with Honey-Sauced Prawns   (page 47)

Classic Hero   (page 62)

Green Bean & Potato Parisienne   (page 68)

Autumn Beef Stew   (page 88)

Fast & Easy Beef Chili Pot   (page 90)

Asian Beef & Noodles   (page 104)

Swiss Steak   (page 126)

Southwestern Corn Soufflé   (page 139)

Mom's Macaroni and Cheese, page 136

Chicken & Rice Caserole, page 20

Hot Out of the Oven

Here they are—those scrumptious covered dishes of yesteryear, right out of Mom's little recipe box. Many are just like you remember them, such as the one with chunks of canned tuna, rich egg noodles, and cream of mushroom soup, all topped with crushed potato chips. Others come with shortcuts on the fixing, but not on the flavor. There are pastas that cook in a flash, cut-up vegetables ready to throw into a dish, and potpies topped with fast biscuits, no piecrust at all. Even salmon bakes the new no-fuss way, inside a foil bag. And potpies are topped off fast with refrigerated biscuits. Take your pick of our one-dish dinners and quickly make one in your oven tonight.

CHICKEN & RICE CASSEROLE

Prep **10 MINUTES**   *Bake* **45 MINUTES + STANDING**

1   can (12 ounces) evaporated milk

1   package (3 ounces) cream cheese, softened

1   can (10¾ ounces) condensed cream of chicken soup

½   cup water

½   teaspoon garlic powder

⅛   teaspoon ground black pepper

1   package (16 ounces) frozen broccoli, cauliflower, and carrot blend, thawed

2   cups cooked chicken, cubed

1½   cups instant rice

2   ounces shredded Cheddar cheese (½ cup)

Who doesn't love a casserole? They're easy to make and can be baked up ahead and reheated.

LET'S BEGIN Preheat the oven to 350°F. Coat a 13 × 9-inch baking dish with cooking spray.

STIR IT TOGETHER Combine the milk and cream cheese in a large bowl and whisk together until well blended. Whisk in the next 4 ingredients until the mixture is smooth. Stir in the vegetables, chicken, and rice.

INTO THE OVEN Transfer the mixture to the baking dish, cover with foil, and bake for 35 minutes. Uncover and sprinkle with the cheese. Bake for 10 to 15 minutes longer, or until bubbling. Let the casserole stand for 5 minutes before serving.

Makes 8 servings

Per serving: 317 calories, 17g protein, 24g carbohydrates, 14g fat, 8g saturated fat, 57mg cholesterol, 478mg sodium

CREAMY TUNA NOODLE CASSEROLE

Prep **15 MINUTES**   *Cook/Bake* **35 MINUTES**

8	ounces medium egg noodles
6	tablespoons butter or margarine
4	stalks celery, chopped
½	cup chopped onion
2	cans (9 ounces each) tuna packed in water, drained and flaked
2	cans (10 ounces each) condensed cream of mushroom soup
1	can (12 ounces) evaporated milk
⅔	cup crushed potato chips

Tuna noodle casserole has been popular for over 50 years. Some versions are topped with toasted bread crumbs or crumbled crackers, but we think nothing beats the taste of crushed potato chips. Enjoy a retro supper: Begin with wedges of iceberg lettuce and blue cheese dressing, and end the meal with chocolate pudding or Jell-O.

LET'S BEGIN Prepare the noodles according to package directions. Drain and keep warm. Preheat the oven to 375°F. Coat a 13 × 9-inch baking dish with cooking spray.

FLASH INTO THE PAN Melt the butter in a large saucepan over medium heat. Add the celery and onion and cook, stirring occasionally, for 1 to 2 minutes, or until vegetables begin to soften. Add the noodles, tuna, soup, and milk and stir to mix well.

INTO THE OVEN Transfer the mixture to the prepared dish and sprinkle the top with the potato chips. Bake for 25 to 30 minutes, or until the chips are golden brown.

Makes 8 servings

Per serving: 454 calories, 23g protein, 34g carbohydrates, 23g fat, 10g saturated fat, 75mg cholesterol, 867mg sodium

EASY CHICKEN AND RICE BAKE

Prep **5 MINUTES** *Bake* **40 MINUTES**

1   **can (14½ ounces) peas and carrots, drained**

1   **can (10¾ ounces) condensed cream of mushroom soup**

¾   **cup white rice**

1   **cup water**

4   **boneless, skinless chicken breast halves (about 1¼ pound)**

    Paprika and ground black pepper (optional)

Chicken and rice can always be counted on to be a fast and tasty crowd-pleaser. Serve with a basket of warm dinner rolls.

LET'S BEGIN Preheat the oven to 400°F. Combine peas and carrots, soup, rice, and water in a large bowl and stir to mix well. Spoon into a 2-quart shallow baking dish and place the chicken over top. Sprinkle with paprika and pepper, if you wish.

INTO THE OVEN Cover and bake for 40 to 45 minutes, or until chicken is cooked through and rice is tender.

Makes 4 servings

Per serving: 370 calories, 32g protein, 42g carbohydrates, 8g fat, 2g saturated fat, 67mg cholesterol, 870mg sodium

SPICY BEEF & BISCUITS

Prep **10 MINUTES**   *Cook* **30 MINUTES**

1   **pound 90% lean ground beef**

1   **small onion, chopped**

4   **teaspoons all-purpose flour**

1   **can (14½ ounces) stewed tomatoes**

⅓   **cup stir-fry sauce**

2   **tablespoons diced canned jalapeño peppers, rinsed and drained**

¼   **cup water**

1½   **cups buttermilk baking mix**

½   **cup milk**

There's real pizzazz in this one-dish dinner—all thanks to canned stewed tomatoes, diced jalapeño peppers, and stir-fry sauce.

LET'S BEGIN Preheat the oven to 425°F. Cook the beef and the onion in a large skillet over medium heat for 6 minutes, or until browned, breaking up the beef with a spoon.

STIR IT IN Add the flour and stir to mix well. Stir in the next 4 ingredients and cook, stirring often, for 3 minutes, or until mixture comes to a boil and thickens slightly. Remove from the heat and cover to keep hot.

INTO THE OVEN Combine baking mix and milk in a medium bowl, stir to form a soft dough, and beat for 30 seconds. Transfer the beef mixture into a 2-quart baking dish and top with rounded teaspoonfuls of the biscuit mixture. Bake for 20 to 25 minutes, or until the biscuits are golden brown.

Makes 4 servings

Per serving: 552 calories, 28g protein, 47g carbohydrates, 27g fat, 10g saturated fat, 82mg cholesterol, 1,611mg sodium

CHEESY TUNA & RICE

Prep **15 MINUTES**   *Cook/Bake* **28 MINUTES**

⅓   cup butter or margarine

1   small onion, chopped

3   tablespoons all-purpose flour

¼   teaspoon salt

⅛   teaspoon ground black pepper

1   can (12 ounces) evaporated milk

6   ounces shredded Cheddar cheese (1½ cups)

2   tablespoons grated Parmesan cheese

1   can (14½ ounces) whole tomatoes, drained and cut in half

1   cup instant rice

1   tablespoon chopped fresh parsley

½   teaspoon paprika

½   teaspoon dried oregano

¼   teaspoon cayenne pepper

2   cans (6 ounces each) tuna packed in water, drained

This easy supper dish is pretty much made from basic pantry ingredients. It's always a good idea to have a couple cans of evaporated milk on hand—for dishes like this favorite and also for a custardy pumpkin pie, even if it isn't Thanksgiving!

LET'S BEGIN Preheat the oven to 375°F. Melt the butter in a medium saucepan. Add the onion and cook for 5 minutes, or until tender. Stir in the flour, salt, and pepper and cook for 1 minute, stirring constantly. Stir in the evaporated milk and cook for 2 minutes, stirring constantly, until mixture comes to a boil. Add the Cheddar and the Parmesan and stir until melted.

STIR IT TOGETHER Combine the next six ingredients in an 11 × 7-inch baking dish and stir to mix well. Top the tomato mixture with the tuna and spread the cheese sauce over the tuna. Bake for 20 to 25 minutes or until bubbling.

Makes 4 servings

Per serving: 683 calories, 43g protein, 42g carbohydrates, 38g fat, 22g saturated fat, 140mg cholesterol, 1,229mg sodium

On the Menu

———◆·✦·◆———

Here's a great brunch—just like you might enjoy in the Deep South. Be sure to bake enough biscuits for folks to have seconds, perhaps even thirds.

———◆·✦·◆———

Cheesy Grits

Country Sausage Patties

Fresh Fruit with Poppy Seed Dressing

Hot Cream Biscuits with Cloverleaf Honey

Iced Tea with Fresh Mint

CHEESY GRITS

Prep **5 MINUTES**   Cook **50 MINUTES + STANDING**

Southerners just love their grits: for breakfast, topped with shrimp, or just the way we've cooked them up here. This is a buttery, cheesy, soul-satisfying casserole that will be impossible to resist—or to have just one helping of. Be sure to use quick-cooking grits to get you out of the kitchen fast.

3	cups water
¾	cup quick-cooking grits
2	cups shredded sharp Cheddar cheese (8 ounces)
¾	cup evaporated milk
⅓	cup butter or margarine, softened
2	large eggs, lightly beaten
¼	teaspoon hot-pepper sauce
⅛	teaspoon ground black pepper

LET'S BEGIN Preheat the oven to 375°F. Coat a 2-quart baking dish with cooking spray.

BUBBLE & STIR Bring the water to a boil in a medium saucepan and slowly stir in the grits. Cover the pan, reduce the heat to low, and simmer, stirring occasionally, for 5 to 6 minutes, or until the water is absorbed and the grits are done. Add 1½ cups of the cheese, the milk, and butter to the saucepan and stir until the cheese and butter melt. Add the eggs, hot-pepper sauce, and black pepper. Stir to mix well.

INTO THE OVEN Transfer mixture to the baking dish and sprinkle the top with the remaining ½ cup of the cheese. Bake for 40 to 45 minutes or until golden brown and puffy. Let stand for 5 minutes for easier serving.

Makes 6 servings

Per serving: 386 calories, 15g protein, 19g carbohydrates, 28g fat, 15g saturated fat, 148mg cholesterol, 371mg sodium

TERRIFIC TUNA TETRAZZINI
Prep **5 MINUTES**   *Cook/Bake* **25 MINUTES**

6   ounces spaghetti

1   jar (16 ounces) creamy
        Alfredo pasta sauce

1   can (6 ounces) tuna in
        water, drained

3   tablespoons garlic herb
        seasoning

¼   cup milk (optional)

**Grated Parmesan cheese
(optional)**

*This is an easy-to-fix version of the classic chicken tetrazzini, which
was created and named for the beloved Italian soprano Luisa
Tetrazzini. Tetrazzini is most often prepared with chicken, though
some believe the original contained turkey.*

LET'S BEGIN Preheat the oven to 400°F. Cook the pasta
according to package directions and drain.

INTO THE OVEN Combine the pasta, sauce, tuna, and
seasoning in a large bowl and stir to mix well. Stir in the milk
to make a thinner sauce, if you wish. Spoon the mixture into a
1½-quart casserole dish and bake for 15 minutes or until
bubbly around the edges and completely heated through.
Sprinkle with the Parmesan, if you like.

Makes 4 servings

*Per serving: 421 calories, 19g protein, 39g carbohydrates,
21g fat, 13g saturated fat, 111mg cholesterol, 1,370mg sodium*

Food Facts

TETRAZZINI: FOOD FOR A SONG BIRD

Luisa Tetrazzini was an Italian
soprano with a magnificent voice.
She made her American debut at
the Metropolitan Opera House in
New York in 1908. She fell so
deeply in love with America that
she became a member of the
Chicago Opera Company during
its 1913–1914 season.

No one knows for sure who
created the first Chicken
Tetrazzini, but it was meant to
honor the beloved opera star. And,
it is believed the dish was first
made in San Francisco, a city that
was enthralled with her voice.

Chicken Tetrazzini is a soul-
satisfying pasta casserole made with

a Parmesan-and-mushroom-
flavored sherry-cream sauce, lots of
chunks of the roasted bird, and a
good amount of spaghetti—all
tossed together, piled into a
casserole, and baked until bubbly.
What better way to enjoy the
music of *Madame Butterfly* or
La Boheme.

CHEESE STEAK PIZZA

Prep **10 MINUTES**   *Cook/Bake* **17 MINUTES**

1   pound 85% lean ground beef

1   small onion, thinly sliced and separated into rings

1   small green or red bell pepper, cut into thin strips

¾   teaspoon salt

½   teaspoon ground black pepper

1   package (16 ounces) prebaked thick pizza crust (12-inch)

2   cups shredded mozzarella cheese (8 ounces)

If you like, you can also make individual pizzas. Let all the "creative" cooks in your family top off their pizzas with favorite toppings, such as sliced mushrooms, halved cherry tomatoes, or broccoli florets.

LET'S BEGIN Preheat the oven to 400°F. Cook the beef in a large nonstick skillet over medium heat for 6 minutes, breaking it up with a spoon. Add the onion and bell pepper and cook 3 minutes, or until beef is not pink and vegetables are crisp-tender, stirring occasionally. Drain off any fat and stir in the salt and pepper.

INTO THE OVEN Place the pizza crust on a baking sheet, top with the beef mixture, then with the cheese. Bake for 8 to 10 minutes, or until cheese melts.

Makes 4 servings

Per serving: 752 calories, 48g protein, 55g carbohydrates, 39g fat, 15g saturated fat, 131mg cholesterol, 1,485mg sodium

VEGETABLE-TOPPED FISH POUCHES

Prep **15 MINUTES + MARINATING**   *Cook* **15 MINUTES**

We love cooking food in a packet. It eliminates the need for pots, the pouches can be put together ahead and refrigerated, and it always impresses. Best yet, there is no need for additional fat—the food steams in its own juices.

4	(4 ounce) flounder, cod, or halibut fillets
1	medium red onion, cut into thin wedges
1	carrot, cut into matchsticks
8	mushrooms, sliced
1	celery stalk, thinly sliced (optional)
1	medium zucchini or yellow squash, thinly sliced (optional)
2	ounces shredded Swiss cheese (½ cup)
½	cup Italian salad dressing

LET'S BEGIN Preheat the broiler or the grill to medium-high. Tear off 4 (9 × 18-inch) pieces of heavy-duty foil and place one fish fillet in the center of each. Top the fish evenly with the onion, carrot, and mushrooms and with the celery and zucchini, if you wish. Top the vegetables evenly with the cheese and the dressing.

FOLD 'EM UP Bring up the foil sides and double fold the top and ends to seal the pouches, leaving room for heat circulation inside. Let the fish stand for 15 minutes.

COOK & SERVE Broil or grill the pouches seam side up for 15 minutes, or until the fish flakes easily when tested with a fork. Wear oven mitts and use a knife to carefully cut open the bag and fold back the top for steam to escape.

Makes 4 servings
Per serving: 258 calories, 26g protein, 9g carbohydrates, 14g fat, 4g saturated fat, 62mg cholesterol, 587mg sodium

Cooking Basics

POUCH COOKING— EASY AS A, B, C!

When it comes to an easy one-dish dinner that's guaranteed to come out perfect every time, pouch cooking can't be beat! They're simple to fill and fold and even easier to clean up (just throw the pouch away). But the best part: The food comes out delicious. All of the flavors slowly simmer and infuse together, creating blue-ribbon results in every bite! Here's all there is to it:

• For each pouch, tear off a large rectangular piece of heavy duty foil, about 9 × 18 inches.

• Place the meat or fish on the bottom, then layer up the vegetables, such as onions, celery, mushrooms, cherry tomatoes, summer squash, or slices of new potatoes—whatever you like. Top with a little butter or olive oil, if you wish, for a little extra flavor.

• Bring up the sides of the foil and double fold them at the top to seal it well—but not too tightly. Be sure to leave enough space for the heat to circulate inside. Then just broil, grill, or bake the pouches according to the recipe. It couldn't be easier! *Bon appétit!*

Savory Salmon Provençal

Prep **15 MINUTES**   *Cook* **14 MINUTES (IF GRILLED) OR 25 MINUTES (IF BAKED)**

1	large foil cooking bag
1	red onion, sliced
6	(4 to 6 ounces) salmon fillets
2	garlic cloves, minced
½	teaspoon salt
¼	teaspoon ground black pepper
1½	teaspoons herbes de Provence or dried salad herbs
2	cups coarsely chopped plum tomatoes
1	jar (6 ounces) marinated artichoke hearts, drained and quartered
⅓	cup pitted Kalamata olives, halved

Herbes de Provence is a blend of herbs that grow wild on the hillsides of southern France and is sold in specialty food stores. It's usually a mix of fennel, rosemary, thyme, lavender, sage, savory, and marjoram—and might make you long for a trip to Nice.

LET'S BEGIN Preheat the grill to medium-high or the oven to 450°F. Place cooking bag in a 1-inch-deep pan. Place onion slices in the bottom of the bag.

LAYER Arrange the salmon skin side down on top of the onion. Sprinkle with garlic, salt, pepper, and ¾ teaspoon of the herbes de Provence. Layer tomatoes, artichoke hearts, and olives over the salmon and sprinkle with the remaining ¾ teaspoon herbes de Provence. Double fold the open end of the bag to seal.

COOK & SERVE Slide the bag onto the grill or leave in the pan and place in the oven. Cook on a covered grill for 14 to 16 minutes, or bake in the oven for 25 to 30 minutes, or until salmon flakes easily when tested with a fork. Wear oven mitts and use a knife to carefully cut open the bag and fold back the top for steam to escape.

Makes 6 servings
Per serving: 269 calories, 35g protein, 9g carbohydrates, 10g fat, 3g saturated fat, 88 mg cholesterol, 553mg sodium

EASY BEEF POTPIE

Prep **15 MINUTES**   *Cook/Bake* **17 MINUTES**

1	**pound boneless beef top sirloin steak, ¾ inch thick**
1	**tablespoon vegetable oil**
½	**pound small mushrooms, quartered**
1	**medium onion, sliced**
¼	**cup water**
1	**clove garlic, minced**
1	**jar (12 ounces) beef gravy**
1	**package (10 ounces) frozen peas and carrots**
¼	**teaspoon dried thyme**
1	**can (4½ ounces) refrigerated buttermilk biscuits**

On a chilly winter night, here's a satisfying beef-and-vegetable pot-pie that's tasty, easy to prepare, and filled with juicy slices of steak.

LET'S BEGIN Preheat the oven to 400°F. Cut the steak lengthwise in half, then cut crosswise into ¼-inch-thick strips.

INTO THE PAN Heat the oil in a large ovenproof skillet over medium-high heat until hot. Add half of the beef and stir-fry for 1 to 2 minutes, or until outside surface of beef is no longer pink. Remove from the skillet and repeat with the remaining beef, adding more oil if necessary.

MAKE IT SAUCY Add the next 4 ingredients to the skillet and cook 3 minutes, or until the onion is tender, stirring often. Stir in gravy, vegetables, and thyme and bring to a boil. Remove from heat; add the beef and stir until well combined. Cut each biscuit into two semicircles. Arrange in a single layer on top of the beef mixture. Bake for 12 to 14 minutes, or until biscuits are golden brown.

Makes 6 servings

Per serving: 310 calories, 21g protein, 21g carbohydrates, 16g fat, 5g saturated fat, 41mg cholesterol, 570mg sodium

---

Time Savers

TOPPING POTPIES FAST!

In Grandma's day, potpies were handmade and always delicious. They often were double-crust pies that took hours to prepare and to watch as they baked. Potpies were a true gesture of love.

Nowadays, you can still serve potpies, even if you don't have hours to make it the old-fashioned way.

Just spoon the filling into a deep pie dish, top it fast, and bake. Our ideas are so easy, why not consider baking one for dinner tonight?

There are plenty of fun ways to top them off, fast and easy:
• Use a package of refrigerated dough to cut out fun shapes of pastry (let the little ones help).

Top the pies with the pastry cutouts and bake until golden and crispy.
• Pipe mashed potatoes over each pie. Bake until puffy and golden.
• Fry up some thin slivers of onion until they're frizzled and crispy. Sprinkle them on the pies right before they go into the oven.

E-Z Street Gumbo, page 43

Skillet Specials

Grab your skillet and get ready to make the fastest, freshest one-dish dinner around. Everything you need for your meal is sautéed, flash-fried, or quickly sauced all in one pan. Turn supper into a Chinese feast with Sweet & Sour Pork or into a Maryland seashore treat with Chesapeake Bay Pasta. Stir up mac 'n' cheese, a hearty chicken stew, or a New Orleans gumbo—all in less than 20 minutes. Thanks to frozen veggies, fast-cooking rice, ready-cleaned seafood, quick-cooking meats, and sauces from a jar, dinner comes straight out of one skillet—often in less than 30 minutes. And the best part is, with all of the conveniences, cleanup is a breeze.

SWEET & SOUR PORK

Prep **10 MINUTES**   *Cook* **10 MINUTES**

½   to ¾ pound boneless pork

1   teaspoon vegetable oil

1   bag (16 ounces) frozen pepper stir-fry vegetable blend

1   tablespoon water

1   jar (14 ounces) sweet and sour sauce

1   can (8 ounces) pineapple chunks, packed in juice, undrained

Hot steamed rice

This classic Chinese-American restaurant dish always gets high ratings. Serve over hot steamed rice. Round out the meal with egg rolls, and don't forget the fortune cookies!

LET'S BEGIN Cut the pork into thin strips. Heat the oil in a large skillet over medium-high heat until hot. Add the pork and stir-fry for 2 to 3 minutes, or until it is lightly browned. Add the vegetables and water and cook, covered, for 5 to 7 minutes, or until vegetables are crisp-tender.

MAKE IT SAUCY Uncover and stir in the sweet and sour sauce and the undrained pineapple chunks. Cook for 3 minutes, or until heated through.

Makes 4 servings

Per serving: 408 calories, 13g protein, 60g carbohydrates, 12g fat, 3g saturated fat, 70mg cholesterol, 300mg sodium

PORK & POTATOES PROVENÇAL

Prep **10 MINUTES**   *Cook* **10 MINUTES**

4   medium potatoes, cut into ¾-inch cubes

1   tablespoon vegetable oil

1   pound lean pork, cut into thin strips

2   cups cherry tomatoes

⅓   cup orange marmalade

2   tablespoons Dijon mustard

Salt and ground black pepper

Thinly sliced pork teams up with potatoes, cherry tomatoes, and an orange sauce to make a dish that's pretty as well as tasty.

LET'S BEGIN Place the potatoes in microwaveable dish and cover with plastic wrap, folding back one corner to vent the steam. Microwave on High for 7 to 8 minutes, or until tender.

SAUTÉ IT QUICKLY Meanwhile, heat the oil in a large skillet over high heat. Add the pork and sauté for 2 to 3 minutes, or until the pork is no longer pink. Drain off any liquid. Add the cooked potatoes and the tomatoes and sauté for 3 minutes, or until tomatoes begin to soften. Add the marmalade and the mustard and toss until marmalade melts. Season to taste with salt and pepper.

Makes 4 servings

Per serving: 375 calories, 25g protein, 46g carbohydrates, 11g fat, 3g saturated fat, 56mg cholesterol, 253mg sodium

STIR-FRIED CHICKEN & RICE

Prep **5 MINUTES**   *Cook* **10 MINUTES**

1   package (8.8 ounces) ready-to-heat rice

1   tablespoon vegetable oil

1   teaspoon minced garlic

½   pound boneless, skinless chicken breast, cut into cubes

2   tablespoons teriyaki or soy sauce

1½   cups frozen Oriental vegetable blend, thawed

Here's a dish that's bursting with flavor! Since it uses ready-to-heat rice from a pouch, it's supper in a flash. Make it with chicken one night, then with cubed boneless pork, shrimp, or cubed beef another. For a traditional touch, scramble two eggs and stir into the rice just before serving.

LET'S BEGIN Prepare the rice according to the package directions, then set aside and keep warm. Meanwhile, heat the oil in a large skillet over medium-high heat. Add the garlic and cook for 1 minute.

STIR-FRY Add the chicken and the sauce and stir-fry for 5 to 7 minutes, or until chicken is cooked through. Stir in the vegetables, cover, and cook for 2 to 3 minutes, or until crisp-tender. Add the rice and toss to combine.

Makes 2 servings

Per serving: 406 calories, 32g protein, 42g carbohydrates, 11g fat, 1g saturated fat, 66mg cholesterol, 1,340mg sodium

---

Time Savers

THE THINNER IT IS, THE FASTER IT COOKS

Want dinner on the table in a hurry? Then pound, pound, pound your way to delicious veal, chicken, or beef cutlets.

POUND IT TENDER The speedy, time-honored technique of pounding meats flattens them into larger, even pieces, so they cook faster and brown more evenly. As the meat flattens, its connective tissues break down, making it more tender with every bite.

PROTECT IT Use a gallon-size resealable freezer bag or clear plastic wrap so you can see exactly what you're doing. Take two sheets of plastic wrap and spray one side of each sheet with nonstick cooking spray. Place the meat you're pounding in the bag or between the sheets, with sprayed sides touching the food. Leave a couple inches of space all around to allow room for spreading.

PICK YOUR TOOL A meat mallet works well—either wooden or stainless steel. Or use a rolling pin (check first that the handles are secure!) or the bottom of a heavy skillet (the cast-iron ones work best).

QUICK & SWIFT Now pound away with a gentle slapping motion, until the cutlet is as thin as you want. Season your cutlets and you're ready to go!

BEEFY VEGETABLE SKILLET

Prep **10 MINUTES**   *Cook* **7 MINUTES**

1¼ pounds boneless beef top sirloin steak, cut ¾ inch thick

2   teaspoons dark sesame oil

2   garlic cloves, minced

1   red bell pepper, cut into thin strips

3   tablespoons reduced-sodium soy sauce, divided

2   tablespoons water

3   cups coarsely chopped fresh spinach

½   cup sliced scallions

3   tablespoons ketchup

Hot cooked rice

This colorful, quick stir-fry is perfect over hot rice, tossed with pasta, or stuffed into a wrap for an Asian-inspired sandwich.

LET'S BEGIN Cut the steak in half lengthwise and then cut crosswise into ¼-inch strips. Place in a large bowl, add the oil and garlic, and toss to coat.

STIR-FRY Heat a large nonstick skillet over medium-high heat until hot. Add half of the steak and stir-fry for 1 to 2 minutes, or until the outside surface is no longer pink. Remove from the skillet and repeat with the remaining steak. Add the bell pepper, 2 tablespoons of the soy sauce, and the water and stir-fry for 2 to 3 minutes, or until the pepper is crisp-tender. Add the spinach and the scallions and stir-fry for 1 minute, or until the spinach wilts.

MAKE IT SAUCY Stir in the ketchup, the remaining 1 tablespoon of soy sauce, and the steak and cook for 2 minutes, stirring constantly until well combined and heated through. Serve the beef and vegetables over rice.

Makes 4 servings

Per serving: 362 calories, 31g protein, 38g carbohydrates, 9g fat, 2g saturated fat, 76mg cholesterol, 751mg sodium

SNAPPIN' BEEF 'N' RICE

Prep **7 MINUTES**   *Cook* **17 MINUTES**

We like sweet Italian sausage links in this dish, but if your family likes food with plenty of bite, use hot Italian sausage instead. When breaking up the meat and sausage, be sure to leave some tempting chunks.

1	pound 85% lean ground beef
2	mild Italian sausages, casings removed, or ¼ pound ground sausage
½	cup chopped onion
1	can (11½ ounces) tomato and chile cocktail drink
1	cup quick-cooking rice (uncooked)
1	can (7 ounces) diced green chiles
1	can (2¼ ounces) sliced ripe olives, drained
½	cup grated Cheddar or Monterey Jack cheese

LET'S BEGIN Cook the beef, sausage, and onion in a large skillet over medium heat for 6 minutes, or until meat is brown, breaking it up with a spoon. Drain off any fat.

STIR IT IN Stir in the tomato cocktail, rice, and chiles and bring to a boil. Reduce the heat, cover, and simmer 10 minutes, or until rice is tender. Stir in the olives and sprinkle with cheese.

Makes 4 servings
Per serving: 570 calories, 32g protein, 31g carbohydrates, 35g fat, 14g saturated fat, 115mg cholesterol, 888mg sodium

---

Cook to Cook

WHEN SHOULD I COVER THE SKILLET?

" Generally, when I'm sautéing, *I work so quickly that I rarely use a cover.*

If pieces are thicker than 1 inch, *cover the skillet during the last few minutes of cooking,* to be sure the food cooks evenly throughout.

When I'm frying food that has coating or breading, such as veal cutlets or fried chicken, I always crisp the food first over high heat. *Then I only partially cover the skillet,* so the center of the food cooks, but the coating stays crisp and doesn't steam.

When you're cooking meat that needs tenderizing, such as round steak, brown it first in a hot skillet over high heat. Then reduce the heat and pour in a liquid containing an acid, such as stewed tomatoes. Cover tightly and let it simmer slowly until the meat's fork-tender.

When poaching fish, I like to bring the liquid to a full boil over high heat. I reduce the heat to low before sliding in the fish. This keeps the fish from falling apart. Then I cover the skillet tightly and let the poaching begin. "

BEEFY RED BEANS & RICE

Prep **15 MINUTES**   *Cook* **26 MINUTES**

1½ cups rice

2 tablespoons vegetable oil

½ pound 85% lean ground beef

1 cup chopped onions

1 cup chopped green bell pepper

1 garlic clove, crushed

1 tablespoon lemon juice

1 tablespoon Creole-style mustard

1 teaspoon cayenne pepper

2 tablespoons soy sauce

1 cup tomato sauce

1 can (19 ounces) kidney beans, rinsed and drained

Red beans and rice is one of Louisiana's most famous contributions to American cuisine. It often contains a bit of ham, bacon, or salt pork for a punch of flavor, which you can add in if you like. Be sure to simmer this dish slowly, just like the locals.

LET'S BEGIN Prepare rice according to package instructions. Meanwhile, heat the oil in a large skillet over medium heat. Add the next 4 ingredients and cook 6 minutes, or until beef is brown, breaking it up with a spoon.

SIMMER SLOW Stir in all the remaining ingredients except the rice, cover, and bring to a boil. Reduce the heat and simmer for 20 minutes. Serve the red beans over hot rice.

Makes 4 servings

Per serving: 618 calories, 25g protein, 89g carbohydrates, 18g fat, 5g saturated fat, 39mg cholesterol, 1,398mg sodium

SUPER SKILLET MAC

Prep **5 MINUTES**   *Cook* **16 MINUTES**

1½ cups macaroni

1   pound 85% lean ground beef

1   cup water

1   can (6 ounces) tomato paste

3   tablespoons sun-dried tomato and herb seasoning blend

Shredded Cheddar cheese (optional)

Rich-tasting tomato paste makes it easy to add tomato to any skillet dish. Elbow macaroni is the classic pasta choice, but any medium tube pasta is fine. The Cheddar cheese is optional, but it adds an extra layer of flavor that can't be beat.

LET'S BEGIN Cook the pasta according to package directions. Drain and keep warm.

FLASH INTO THE PAN Meanwhile, cook the beef in a large skillet over medium heat for 6 minutes, or until browned. Drain off any fat. Stir in the pasta and the next 3 ingredients. Cook 3 minutes, or until hot. Top with cheese if you wish.

Makes 5 servings

Per serving: 336 calories, 23g protein, 34g carbohydrates, 12g fat, 5g saturated fat, 56mg cholesterol, 457mg sodium

CREAMY SKILLET TURKEY

Prep **10 MINUTES**   *Cook* **6 MINUTES**

2	teaspoons vegetable oil
3	cups diced cooked turkey, chicken, or ham
½	teaspoon dried thyme (optional)
1	can (10¾ ounces) condensed cream of mushroom soup
½	cup milk
1	can (14½ ounces) cut green beans, drained

Cream of mushroom soup adds lots of flavor without a lot of work. Buy deli roast chicken or turkey, or cut up a ham steak, if you prefer.

LET'S BEGIN Heat the oil in a large skillet over medium-high heat. Add the turkey and thyme, and cook 3 minutes, or until heated through.

MAKE IT SAUCY Stir together the soup and the milk in a small bowl and add to the skillet along with the green beans. Cook 3 minutes, or until heated through. To serve, spoon over hot buttered noodles, mashed potatoes, or hot biscuits, if you wish.

Makes 4 servings

Per serving: 190 calories, 16g protein, 12g carbohydrates, 8g fat, 2g saturated fat, 29mg cholesterol, 1,675mg sodium

---

Food Facts

MAKING SKILLET DINNERS HEALTHIER

Naturally, a healthy skillet begins with the freshest and the best quality ingredients you can find. Here are the steps you can take to make the skillet healthier than it started out:

1. Drizzle in the oil, no butter, please! When sautéing, a little fat is often called for to start the cooking. Reach for olive oil or canola oil, not butter or margarine. These oils are heart healthy—that is, high in monounsaturated fats, "zero" cholesterol, and low in saturated and trans fats.

Tip: No need to use an expensive extra-virgin olive oil (first pressing) in the skillet, as heat breaks down the extra fruity flavor. Choose a more affordable pure olive oil for the skillet instead.

2. Go for lean! When buying ground meat, reach for the leanest one you can find, usually ground sirloin, at least 90% lean. This keeps the fat content of the skillet down.

3. Forget the skin. Choose skinless chicken breasts for the skillet to keep the fat and calories low.

4. Rinse away! When adding canned beans to the skillet, drain and rinse them first. This lowers the sodium content. Remember, beans are a great way to increase the fiber in a dish.

5. Go for light and low! Choose light soy sauce and low-sodium canned tomato products to keep the sodium down. Add a few tiny pinches of salt to the skillet to sparkle the flavors, if you wish.

6. Sprinkle on the nuts! Add great texture plus heart-healthy fats and other vitamins, minerals, and fiber to the skillet by stirring in almonds or walnuts.

SuperQuick
TURKEY DIJON

Prep **5 MINUTES**   *Cook* **18 MINUTES**

1	tablespoon butter or margarine
1	pound turkey cutlets
1	cup frozen mixed vegetables
1	box (10 ounces) frozen onions with cream sauce
1	teaspoon spicy brown mustard

Use any favorite blend of frozen mixed vegetables in this easy one-skillet dinner. We like the flavor of spicy brown mustard, but Dijon also adds a good zesty flavor. If you can't find turkey cutlets in the meat case, chicken cutlets will also do the trick.

LET'S BEGIN Heat the butter in a large nonstick skillet over medium-high heat. Cook the turkey 8 minutes, turning once, until browned on both sides.

SIMMER & SERVE Add the remaining ingredients and bring to a boil. Reduce the heat to medium-low, cover, and simmer 6 to 8 minutes, or until vegetables are tender.

> *Makes 4 servings*
>
> *Per serving: 218 calories, 28g protein, 7g carbohydrates, 5g fat, 3g saturated fat, 55mg cholesterol, 600mg sodium*

SuperQuick
HEARTY CHICKEN STEW

Prep **8 MINUTES**   *Cook* **8 MINUTES**

1	jar (12 ounces) chicken gravy
¼	teaspoon leaf sage, crushed, or poultry seasoning
6	ounces cooked chicken chunks (about 1 cup)
1	can (8 ounces) cut green beans, drained
1	can (8¼ ounces) sliced carrots, drained
2	to 3 corn sticks or corn muffins, warmed and halved

This tasty skillet meal captures some of the best flavors of Thanksgiving: cornbread, gravy, sage, and green beans. In fact, this dish is a great way to use up any of the leftover holiday bird.

LET'S BEGIN Combine gravy and sage in a large skillet and bring to a boil over medium heat.

MAKE IT SAUCY Add the chicken, beans, and carrots and cook 3 minutes, or until heated through.

SERVE To serve, spoon the stew over corn sticks or corn muffin halves.

> *Makes 2 servings*
>
> *Per serving: 614 calories, 35g protein, 57g carbohydrates, 27g fat, 6g saturated fat, 100mg cholesterol, 2,125mg sodium*

E–Z Street Gumbo

Prep **5 minutes**   *Cook* **15 minutes**

½   **pound smoked sausage, thinly sliced**

1   **can (14½ ounces) stewed tomatoes**

1   **box (10 ounces) frozen mixed vegetables, thawed**

2   **tablespoons Cajun seasoning**

½   **pound medium cooked, peeled, and deveined shrimp**

Hot cooked rice

One taste of this gumbo will have you thinking you're in the Big Easy. Gumbo is a mainstay of New Orleans cuisine. We love the easy flavor-filled one that's ready in 20 minutes. Substitute chicken or beef cubes for sausage. Add okra for authenticity. Ladle the gumbo over scoops of hot rice in large, shallow soup bowls.

LET'S BEGIN Heat a large nonstick skillet over medium-high heat. Add the sausage and cook for 3 minutes, stirring often, until lightly browned. Stir in the tomatoes, vegetables and the seasoning and bring to a boil. Reduce the heat, cover, and simmer for 10 minutes.

BUBBLE & STIR Stir in the shrimp and cook 2 to 3 minutes, just until heated through. Serve with rice.

Makes 4 servings

Per serving: 368 calories, 28g protein, 19g carbohydrates, 20g fat, 7g saturated fat, 149mg cholesterol, 1,792mg sodium

COUNTRY PORK SKILLET

Prep **10 MINUTES**   *Cook* **25 MINUTES**

4   **boneless pork chops, about 1 pound, diced**

1   **jar (12 ounces) pork gravy**

2   **tablespoons ketchup**

8   **small red potatoes, diced**

2   **cups frozen mixed vegetables**

Cut down on your kitchen time by using pre-diced potatoes from the refrigerated produce case. Round out the meal with a leafy green lettuce salad with sliced apples and scallions, tossed with your favorite vinaigrette. Pass plenty of biscuits, hot out of the oven.

LET'S BEGIN Heat a large nonstick skillet over medium-high heat. Add the pork and cook for 5 minutes, stirring often, until well-browned. Stir in the gravy, ketchup, and potatoes. Reduce the heat, cover, and simmer for 10 minutes.

SIMMER LOW Stir in the mixed vegetables and simmer for 10 to 15 minutes longer, or until vegetables are tender.

Makes 4 servings

Per serving: 430 calories, 33g protein, 52g carbohydrates, 12g fat, 4g saturated fat, 70mg cholesterol, 690mg sodium

SuperQuick
FAT TUESDAY NOODLES

Prep **15 MINUTES**   *Cook* **15 MINUTES**

When it comes to fast, angel hair pasta is the way to go. This ultra-thin pasta takes only minutes to go from uncooked to al dente. This dish is big on flavor, and it contains the holy trinity of classic Creole cuisine: chopped onion, celery, and green bell pepper.

1	tablespoon olive oil
½	cup chopped onion
½	cup chopped celery
½	cup chopped green bell pepper
1½	teaspoons dried Italian seasoning
½	teaspoon red-pepper flakes
½	teaspoon coarse ground black pepper
½	pound smoked or andouille sausage
½	pound large shrimp, peeled and deveined
4	cups chicken broth
8	ounces capellini (angel hair pasta)

LET'S BEGIN Heat the olive oil in a large skillet over medium-high heat. Add the onion, celery, and bell pepper and cook for 8 minutes, or until tender, stirring often. Stir in the Italian seasoning, red-pepper flakes, and black pepper.

BUBBLE & STIR Meanwhile, cut the sausage in half lengthwise and then cut it into ½-inch slices. Add the sausage and the shrimp to the skillet and cook for 2 minutes, stirring often, or until shrimp begin to turn pink. Add the chicken broth and bring to a boil. Break the pasta in half and add to the skillet. Cook for 3 to 5 minutes, or until the pasta is done.

Makes 7 servings

Per serving: 313 calories, 18g protein, 29g carbohydrates, 14g fat, 4g saturated fat, 64mg cholesterol, 765mg sodium

---

Cook to Cook

HOW CAN I SPEED UP THE SKILLET?

" *Cut up all the ingredients first before turning on the heat.* That way, once you start cooking, you won't lose time.

Always defrost meat and poultry completely before adding it to the skillet.

Heat up the skillet with a little oil before adding the food. This gets the food cooking right away.

Cook rice or pasta separately, then toss into the skillet during the last few minutes before the dish is done.

Microwave or steam potatoes before adding them to the skillet. This prevents the other ingredients from overcooking while potatoes do their cooking.

Cut vegetables small and in similar-size pieces. When adding raw vegetables, such as carrots and celery, first blanch them in boiling water for a few minutes, just until their color brightens. Then when you toss them into the skillet, they'll start cooking right away. "

CHESAPEAKE BAY PASTA

Prep **10 MINUTES**   *Cook* **17 MINUTES**

8	ounces penne
1	pound boneless, skinless chicken breasts, cut in ½-inch strips
4	teaspoons Old Bay seasoning
1	tablespoon butter
½	pound large shrimp, peeled and deveined
1	cup heavy cream
3	scallions, sliced

Heavy cream adds a welcome richness to this elegant and easy skillet dish. If you prefer a lighter rendition, use light cream or half-and-half instead. For an extra touch of color, buy presliced red bell pepper and add about ½ cup along with the scallions.

LET'S BEGIN Cook the pasta according to package directions. Drain and keep warm.

FLASH INTO THE PAN Meanwhile, sprinkle the chicken evenly on both sides with 2 teaspoons of the seasoning. Melt the butter in a large nonstick skillet over medium heat. Add the chicken and cook for 3 minutes, stirring often. Coat the shrimp with 1 teaspoon of the remaining seasoning. Push the chicken to one side of the skillet and add the shrimp. Cook for 3 to 4 minutes or until the shrimp turn pink, stirring constantly.

MAKE IT SAUCY Combine the cream and the remaining 1 teaspoon of the seasoning in a small bowl and stir to mix well. Add the cream mixture, pasta, and scallions to the skillet and bring to a boil. Lower the heat and simmer for 5 minutes, or until the sauce thickens and pasta is heated through.

Makes 5 servings

Per serving: 517 calories, 37g protein, 36g carbohydrates, 25g fat, 13g saturated fat, 207mg cholesterol, 578mg sodium

LINGUINI WITH HONEY-SAUCED PRAWNS

Prep **15 MINUTES**   *Cook* **15 MINUTES**

1	pound linguini
½	cup water
¼	cup honey
4	teaspoons cornstarch
¼	teaspoon dried rosemary
¼	teaspoon red-pepper flakes
1	teaspoon salt
1	large carrot
1	celery stalk
2	tablespoons olive oil
1	pound prawns, peeled and deveined
½	cup diagonally sliced scallions
3	garlic cloves, minced

The combination of honey and red-pepper flakes in this dish makes it a real winner. Prawns are very large shrimp. There are fewer per pound, which means faster peeling and deveining. Cut the vegetables into matchsticks fast by using a vegetable slicer.

LET'S BEGIN Cook the pasta according to package directions. Drain and keep warm. Combine the next 6 ingredients in a small bowl and set aside. Cut the carrot and celery into matchsticks.

STIR-FRY Meanwhile, heat the oil in a large nonstick wok or skillet over medium-high heat. Stir-fry the prawns, carrot, celery, scallions, and garlic for 3 minutes, or until prawns start to turn pink. Add the honey mixture and stir-fry for 1 minute, or until the sauce boils and thickens. Serve over linguini.

Makes 4 servings

Per serving: 445 calories, 27g protein, 66g carbohydrates, 8g fat, 1g saturated fat, 220mg cholesterol, 718mg sodium

LEMON SHRIMP RICE

Prep **10 MINUTES**   *Cook* **20 MINUTES**

1	package (8.8 ounces) bistro long grain rice
1	tablespoon butter or margarine
½	pound medium shrimp, peeled and deveined
½	cup diced red bell pepper
½	cup sliced scallions
1	teaspoon minced garlic
1	tablespoon lemon juice
¼	cup chopped cilantro

Lemon wedges

Cilantro leaves

Fresh lemon juice and minced fresh garlic add just the right burst of flavor. Here's the fastest way to peel garlic. Lightly smack the clove with the side of a large knife. The skin pops right off. Chop off the stem end and mince away.

LET'S BEGIN Prepare the rice according to package directions and keep warm.

FLASH INTO THE PAN Meanwhile, heat the butter in a large skillet over medium-high heat. Add the next 5 ingredients and cook for 3 to 5 minutes, stirring constantly, until the shrimp turn pink. Stir in the chopped cilantro, cover, and let stand for 1 minute. Serve the shrimp over the rice. Garnish with lemon wedges and cilantro leaves.

Makes 2 servings

Per serving: 380 calories, 28g protein, 43g carbohydrates, 11g fat, 3g saturated fat, 188mg cholesterol, 861mg sodium

---

Cooking Basics

SAUTÉING 101

Start with dry! Wet ingredients will steam, instead of brown, turning beef a gray color. Keep the surfaces of very moist ingredients, dry by dusting them with flour first.

Just a little oil. Use only enough oil to coat the skillet with a thin film, about ¹⁄₁₆ inch, and heat before adding the food.

No overcrowding, please! If you add too much food to the skillet, the temperature drops and food steams instead of browns. **Tip:** If you can't see the bottom of the

skillet between pieces of food, take some out and cook in batches.

Let it cook. To brown food better, let it cook on its own for a few minutes before turning.

Shake and flip! When sautéing vegetables, use a nonstick skillet with sloping sides and enough fat to let the food move around the skillet. First, tilt the skillet, letting the food slide away from you (# 1). Then quickly jerk the handle down. With a snappy "jumpy" motion, flip the food back toward the center of

the pan (# 2). Keep flipping the until food is cooked to your liking.

#1

#2

ZIPPY ZITI

Prep **5 MINUTES**   *Cook* **15 MINUTES**

8   ounces ziti, mostaccioli (moustaches), or other medium pasta shape

1½   tablespoons vegetable oil

2   scallions, finely chopped

½   cup skim milk

4   ounces shredded Cheddar cheese (1 cup)

2   tablespoons horseradish sauce

½   teaspoon dried Italian seasoning

1½   cups cooked mixed vegetables

Salt and ground black pepper

Horseradish sauce adds good-tasting zip to this fabulous dish. Serve it with lots of warm garlic bread and a tomato and cucumber salad, with Italian dressing on the side. For dessert, pick up cannoli or ricotta cheese pie—oh so good!

LET'S BEGIN Cook the pasta according to package directions, drain and set aside to keep warm.

MAKE IT SAUCY Meanwhile, heat the oil in a large skillet over medium heat. Add the scallions and sauté 3 minutes or until softened. Add the milk, then add the cheese, horseradish sauce, and Italian seasoning and cook 3 minutes, or until cheese melts, stirring constantly.

TOSS IT UP Add the vegetables and cook 3 minutes, or until heated through. Season to taste with salt and pepper. Toss the pasta and the sauce in a large bowl.

Makes 4 servings

Per serving: 431 calories, 17g protein, 54g carbohydrates, 16g fat, 7g saturated fat, 31mg cholesterol, 298mg sodium

SPICY PORK NOODLES

Prep **15 MINUTES**   *Cook* **12 MINUTES**

2	tablespoons Worcestershire sauce
1	tablespoon soy sauce
2	teaspoons cornstarch
½	teaspoon curry powder
2	tablespoons vegetable oil
1	pound lean pork (shoulder, fresh ham, or tenderloin), cut into ¼-inch thick strips
1	medium onion, thinly sliced
8	ounces broccoli florets
2	cups cooked linguini, warm
1	tomato, chopped

Like most Chinese food, leftovers of this dish are delicious. It may seem a bit surprising to see curry powder in a recipe for Chinese food, but it is not as unusual as you might think. Curry powder can contain up to 20 different spices, which adds up to great-tasting food.

LET'S BEGIN Combine the first 4 ingredients in a small bowl, stir until well mixed, and set aside. Heat 1 tablespoon of the oil in a wok or a large skillet over high heat. Add the pork and stir-fry for 6 to 7 minutes, or until lightly browned. Remove from the wok and set aside. Add the remaining oil to the wok, then add the onion and broccoli and stir-fry for 4 to 5 minutes, or until crisp-tender.

MAKE IT SAUCY Add the Worcestershire mixture to the wok and cook for 1 minute, stirring constantly, until slightly thickened. Return the pork to the wok and cook 1 minute longer, or until heated through.

TOSS IT UP Combine the linguine, tomato, and the pork and vegetable mixture in a large serving bowl and toss to combine.

Makes 4 servings

Per serving: 372 calories, 29g protein, 30g carbohydrates, 15g fat, 4g saturated fat, 110mg cholesterol, 477mg sodium

PARMESAN NOODLE SKILLET

Prep **15 MINUTES**   *Cook* **15 MINUTES**

2   cups medium egg
    noodles

12 ounces 85% lean ground
    beef

1   cup light Alfredo pasta
    sauce

2   tablespoons water

1   can (14½ ounces) whole
    green beans, drained

¼   cup chopped red bell
    pepper

Grated Parmesan cheese
    (optional)

Alfredo di Lello, a restaurant owner in Italy during the 1920s, created Fettuccine Alfredo. The dish became an immediate hit. Here, a lower-calorie version of the sauce is combined with noodles, green beans, and ground beef for a satisfying skillet meal.

LET'S BEGIN Cook the noodles according to package directions. Drain and keep warm.

MAKE IT SAUCY Meanwhile, cook the beef in a large nonstick skillet over medium heat for 6 minutes, or until brown, breaking it up with a spoon. Drain off any fat. Stir in the cooked noodles, sauce, and water and cook 3 minutes, or until heated through.

STIR & HEAT Stir in the green beans and bell pepper and cook 3 minutes, or until heated through. Sprinkle with cheese, if you wish.

Makes 4 servings

Per serving: 375 calories, 22g protein, 22g carbohydrates, 21g fat, 10g saturated fat, 102mg cholesterol, 770mg sodium

Cooking Basics

PICKING THE RIGHT SKILLET

With such a wide range of skillets available, it can be daunting to choose one. But cooking with the right skillet can make all the difference between good food and fabulous food. So here are some tips when shopping for a skillet.

• **Heavy skillets.** They take a bit longer to heat up but retain heat well and cook food evenly. Enameled cast iron, black cast iron, and heavy-bottomed aluminum and stainless steel are all good choices. Some come with nonstick coatings.

• **How to know when a pan's handle is good?** Simply pick up the skillet and check out how it feels in your hand. It should fit nicely and feel comfortable. Metal handles are great because they are also oven-safe. They are often sold with rubber sleeves to protect you when they are hot.

• **Skillet sides.** Some are straight-sided and others are sloping. Large, deep, straight-sided skillets are perfect for frying and for one-dish meals. Slope-sided pans are excellent for sautéing, omelets, and pan sauces. Their flared shape encourages the rapid evaporation of liquid, giving food rich color.

CATFISH 'N' PASTA
Prep **15 MINUTES**   *Cook* **5 MINUTES**

8	ounces capellini (angel hair pasta)
2	(6-ounce) catfish fillets
3	tablespoons butter
1	cup frozen artichoke hearts, thawed and thinly sliced
1	red bell pepper, cut into matchsticks
1	carrot, cut into matchsticks
1	zucchini, cut into matchsticks
⅔	cup heavy cream or milk

Salt and ground black pepper

½	cup grated Parmesan cheese
¼	teaspoon ground nutmeg

Even people who shy away from eating fish will love this dish. Catfish is a mild-tasting, non-oily fish. The addition of heavy cream makes it enticingly rich.

LET'S BEGIN Cook the pasta according to package directions. Drain and keep warm in a large serving bowl.

FLASH INTO THE PAN Meanwhile, cut the catfish fillets in half crosswise and slice into thin strips. Heat the butter in a large skillet over medium heat. Add the catfish and cook for 1 minute, stirring constantly. Stir in the next four ingredients and cook for 3 minutes, or until the vegetables are crisp-tender and the fish flakes easily when tested with a fork. Stir in the cream and season to taste with salt and pepper.

TOSS IT UP Pour the catfish mixture over the pasta, sprinkle with the Parmesan and toss. Sprinkle with nutmeg.

Makes 4 servings

Per serving: 630 calories, 28g protein, 53g carbohydrates, 35g fat, 17g saturated fat, 128mg cholesterol, 393mg sodium

Thai Turkey Sandwiches, page 70

Salad & Sandwich Corner

Surprise! Salads and sandwiches really are one-dish dinners too! The reason is quite simple: They go together in one bowl or plate and blend together to make a great-tasting treat, more delicious than their individual parts. It's all thanks to the perfect mix of ingredients, dressings, and sauces. So get out your salad bowl and chop up a California Cobb, spice up a chicken salad with curry, or fix a summer tuna salad fast. Toss up that favorite Caesar salad, then find out how the very first one was created. Another day, grill a burger or overstuff a hero. Then wait a few minutes to let the flavors blend, and get ready to take a delicious big bite!

4 FAST SALAD TOSSES

Pick up a bag of ready-to-serve salad mix, a bottle of vinaigrette, and try one of these tasty no-cook supper suggestions.

NIÇOISE SALAD MIX
Reach for a can of tuna, and then pile on green beans, ready-cooked diced potatoes, cherry tomatoes, and wedges of hard-cooked egg.

MEDITERRANEAN SALAD MIX
Add your favorite beans (canned are just fine), sliced fresh white mushrooms, diced roasted peppers, olives, capers, and drained marinated artichoke hearts to the salad. Sprinkle with freshly grated Parmesan.

SHRIMP SALAD MIX
Toss in some cooked shrimp (thawed frozen are great!), corn niblets, chopped plum tomatoes, red onion, and a handful of chopped cilantro.

BEEF SALAD MIX
Mix the salad with ready-cooked seasoned beef strips, sliced red onion, cherry tomatoes, and hearty chunks of blue cheese. Toss it up with vinaigrette and serve.

CURRIED CHICKEN SALAD

Prep **15 MINUTES + CHILLING**

This chicken salad takes a blue ribbon! The apple, celery, and cashews add crunch, raisins add a touch of sweetness, and curry powder contributes just the right mix of heat and spice. Serve on crisp leaf lettuce with heated pita triangles and tall glasses of minted iced tea.

1	cup mayonnaise
2	teaspoons curry powder
3	cups cooked diced chicken
1	Granny Smith apple, chopped
1	cup diced celery
¼	cup cashews
½	cup raisins

FIX IT FAST Combine the mayonnaise and curry powder in a large bowl and stir to mix well. Stir in the remaining ingredients.

LET IT CHILL Cover and refrigerate at least 30 minutes before serving.

Makes 8 servings

Per serving: 361 calories, 16g protein, 13g carbohydrates, 28g fat, 5g saturated fat, 57mg cholesterol, 239mg sodium

STRAWBERRY TURKEY SALAD

Prep **20 MINUTES + CHILLING**

½ cup light mayonnaise

2 tablespoons mango chutney, finely chopped

1 teaspoon grated lime zest

1 tablespoon lime juice

1 teaspoon curry powder

2 cups chopped smoked turkey

1 cup sliced celery

¼ cup diced red onion

Salt

1½ pints fresh strawberries

Lettuce leaves

Mint sprigs

Fix turkey salad the true West Coast way, with fresh strawberries. Available year-round, California strawberries can always be counted on to be brightly colored, juicy, and full of flavor.

LET'S BEGIN Combine first 5 ingredients in a large bowl and stir to mix well. Add the turkey, celery, and onion and toss to coat. Season to taste with salt, cover, and refrigerate for several hours until thoroughly chilled or overnight.

TOSS & SERVE Just before serving, slice 1 pint of the strawberries, add to the turkey mixture, and toss gently to combine. Line a platter with lettuce leaves and spoon the turkey salad into the center. Arrange the remaining strawberries around the salad and garnish with mint.

Makes 4 servings

Per serving: 221 calories, 15g protein, 16g carbohydrates, 11g fat, 2g saturated fat, 41mg cholesterol, 1,200mg sodium

Cooking Basics

SALAD ART

A great salad is composed of different ingredients with varying textures and colors that complement each other in the salad bowl: leafy greens, meats, grains, fruits, nuts, or cheeses. The choice is yours!

GO FOR THE GREENS

Salad greens are not always green—they also come in all shades of reds, purples, yellows, whites, and even browns.

Green Greens: Boston, iceberg, green leaf, red leaf, romaine

Baby Lettuces: baby bibb (green or red), Lola Rosa (frilly), pirate, red sails

Mesclun: a mixture of several baby lettuces

Arugula, also known as rocket: strong spicy, peppery flavor

Endive: Belgian (white), curly (green), escarole (broad leaf)—slightly bitter flavor

Mâche: lamb's lettuce—tiny leaves with a delicate flavor

Radicchio: looks like a small red cabbage—has a bitter taste

Spinach: rich flavor and fairly crisp

Watercress: dime-size leaves with peppery and spicy taste

FRESH HERBS AND EDIBLE FLOWERS

Many herbs go great in salads. Consider basil, cilantro, dill, marjoram, mint, oregano, sage, tarragon, and thyme. Edible flowers are pretty and brightly colored. For tossing into salads, look for nasturtiums, pansies, roses, squash blossoms, violets.

SOUTHWESTERN CHICKEN SALAD

Prep **20 MINUTES**

1   head Boston, red leaf, or romaine lettuce

2   cups cooked or smoked chicken, shredded or diced

1   red bell pepper, thinly sliced

1   ripe avocado, peeled, pitted, and diced

1   ripe mango, peeled and diced

1   small red onion, thinly sliced

1   cup canned black beans, rinsed and drained

¾   cup Chipotle-Honey Sauce (see recipe)

Personalize this beautiful salad by using your favorite lettuce and orange bell peppers. Be sure to use ripe mango and avocado for the best flavor. They are ripe when they yield to gentle pressure.

LET'S BEGIN Tear the lettuce into bite-size pieces and place in a large serving bowl. Add all the remaining ingredients except the sauce.

TOSS & SERVE Prepare the Chipotle-Honey Sauce. Drizzle ¾ cup sauce over the salad and gently toss to coat. Serve salad immediately.

CHIPOTLE-HONEY SAUCE

In a medium bowl, whisk together 1 canned chipotle pepper in adobo sauce, minced; 1½ tablespoons minced fresh ginger; 2 teaspoons minced garlic; ¼ cup soy sauce; 3 tablespoons lemon juice; 3 tablespoons orange juice; and 1 tablespoon honey. Slowly whisk in ¾ cup olive oil. The recipe makes about 1½ cups of sauce. Refrigerate the leftovers for up to 1 week and use as a marinade for chicken thighs or pork, or serve it over baked or grilled fish.

Makes 4 servings
Per serving: 518 calories, 27g protein, 32g carbohydrates, 32g fat, 5g saturated fat, 62mg cholesterol, 592mg sodium

GALA SALAD TOSS

Prep 15 MINUTES

1	head iceberg lettuce, torn
1	pound cooked turkey or chicken, cubed
1	tomato, cut into 8 wedges
1	green or red bell pepper, chopped
3	scallions, sliced
½	cup sliced celery
1	cup seasoned croutons
½	cup blue cheese dressing

Here's how to pick the best head of iceberg lettuce. Choose a head that has lots of leafy outer green leaves. Give the lettuce a little squeeze—it should give slightly, not be hard as a rock. To quickly remove the core, smack the core hard on the counter, then simply twist and pull. To separate leaves, run water through the center and pull apart gently.

FIX IT FAST Arrange the first 6 ingredients in a large salad bowl. Add the croutons and the dressing and toss to coat.

Makes 6 servings

Per serving: 283 calories, 25g protein, 10g carbohydrates, 16g fat, 4g saturated fat, 61mg cholesterol, 378mg sodium

---

Cook to Cook

HOW CAN I TURN A SALAD INTO A SATISFYING SUPPER?

"I love to create robust main-dish salads that contain unexpected combinations of ingredients. Here are five of my favorite.

Make a Club Sandwich Salad by combining lots of torn iceberg lettuce, tomato wedges, chunky croutons, and shredded deli chicken. Toss with any favorite creamy dressing and top with lots of crispy, crunchy bacon bits.

The classic Mediterranean mix of sliced fresh fennel, orange slices, thinly sliced red onion, and brine-cured black olives is a truly refreshing feast. Season it up with salt, pepper, olive oil, and a quick drizzle of red wine vinegar. Top it off with freshly grilled shrimp, and dinner is ready.

Here's a fruity combination that is unusual and absolutely delicious. Combine chopped shallot, halved and thinly sliced Fuyu persimmon (the kind that is ripe when firm), a generous amount of curly endive (also known as frisee), and a thinly sliced medium tart apple. Some honey vinaigrette and turkey chunks make it complete.

Make a tuna unmelt by mixing green leaf lettuce, thinly sliced tomato, torn white bread toast, drained and flaked tuna, and shredded Swiss cheese together in a salad bowl. Serve with Thousand Island Dressing and potato chips.

Make a *special Greek salad* during the warm weather by combining thickly sliced cucumber and red onion, black olives, halved cherry tomatoes, torn Boston or romaine lettuce, and rough chunks of mild feta cheese. Topped off with sliced grilled flank steak and drizzled with a lemony dressing, it's a meal fit for a Greek god (or goddess)."

CAESAR SALAD

Prep **15 MINUTES**   *Cook* **8 MINUTES**

1   envelope (1.02 ounces) dry Caesar salad dressing mix

¼   cup lemon juice

1   pound boneless, skinless chicken breast halves, cut into strips

6   cups torn romaine lettuce

1   cup seasoned croutons

⅓   cup shredded Parmesan cheese

Lemon wedges (optional)

Caesar salad dressing mix makes preparing this classic salad a breeze—and you know it'll taste just like the original one. For the best flavor, buy already-grated cheese at a specialty food store.

LET'S BEGIN Prepare the salad dressing mix according to package directions, using the lemon juice instead of vinegar. Combine the chicken and 1 tablespoon of the prepared dressing in a large nonstick skillet. Cook over medium heat for 8 minutes, stirring often, until chicken is cooked through.

TOSS IT UP Combine the chicken, lettuce, croutons, and Parmesan in a large salad bowl. Add the remaining dressing and toss to coat. Serve with lemon wedges, if you wish.

Makes 6 servings

Per serving: 380 calories, 24g protein, 10g carbohydrates, 27g fat, 5g saturated fat, 60mg cholesterol, 687mg sodium

Food Facts

THE TALE OF THE FIRST CAESAR SALAD

The year was 1924. During those days, Hollywood movie stars frequently headed south across the Mexican border for fun nights on the town. Tijuana was a popular stop—especially a restaurant named Caesar's Palace.

As the tale is told, on the evening of July 24, 1924, owner Caesar Cardini had so many guests that he almost ran out of food. Since the local stores were already closed, he went into his food storeroom to see what was there.

The pickings were slim but good: several crates of romaine (considered a delicacy in those days), a slab of Romano cheese, some bottles of excellent olive oil, and half a crate of eggs.

He quickly began putting together a salad using lots of crisp romaine and grated Romano. Then he rubbed a salad bowl with garlic and tossed up the salad with a lemony dressing. But he wasn't quite done. He coddled an egg (just for a minute) and added it to the salad. This made the dressing stick to the greens.

Cardini believed that since his guests were show people, they would like some entertainment. So he sent out his dining room captains to dramatically create the salad at the guests' tables. His movie guests were so impressed that they didn't order anything else. Immediately, a classic salad was born, and its fame quickly spread across the country.

CALIFORNIA COBB SALAD

Prep **20 MINUTES**

8   cups torn romaine lettuce

2   cups cubed cooked
     chicken

2   cups cherry tomatoes,
     halved

4   hard-cooked eggs, cut
     into wedges

1   avocado, chopped

4   slices bacon, cooked and
     crumbled

¾   cup creamy blue cheese
     salad dressing with
     gorgonzola

Cobb salad is truly a California classic. It was created in 1937 at the Brown Derby restaurant in Hollywood from odds and ends that owner Bob Cobb threw together for one of his buddies late one night after the kitchen had closed. The rest is history—delicious-eating history.

FIX IT FAST Arrange the lettuce on a large serving platter. Top with the next 5 ingredients and drizzle with the dressing.

Makes 4 servings

Per serving: 576 calories, 34g protein, 14g carbohydrates, 44g fat, 9g saturated fat, 290mg cholesterol, 787mg sodium

HEARTY SUMMER SALAD

Prep **15 MINUTES**

1   small head iceberg
     lettuce, torn

4   cups torn romaine lettuce

2   cans (7 ounces each)
     tuna packed in water,
     drained, and flaked

8   ounces mushrooms,
     sliced

2   tomatoes, each cut into
     8 wedges

1   green or yellow bell
     pepper, cut into rings

¾   cup Italian or French
     dressing

You know it's summer, when there's time for those leisurely luncheons on the terrace. This colorful and tasty mix of vegetables makes the perfect entreé—all flavored up with Italian or French dressing. Use iceberg and romaine lettuce for their appealing crunch, or feel free to experiment with any lettuce you like.

FIX IT FAST Arrange the first 6 ingredients in a large salad bowl. Add the dressing and toss to coat.

Makes 6 servings

Per serving: 200 calories, 20g protein, 9g carbohydrates, 10g fat, 2g saturated fat, 20mg cholesterol, 722mg sodium

SuperQuick
CLASSIC HERO

Prep **10 MINUTES**

Hero sandwiches are classics for good reason—they are fast to fix and simply oh-so-delicious! Here, the bread soaks up all the tasty dressing, which softens the bread a bit, while shredded iceberg lettuce adds lots of welcome crunch. Shred the lettuce up to a couple of days ahead and store in the fridge in a plastic bag.

½   **cup salad dressing or light mayonnaise**

1   **teaspoon dried Italian seasoning**

1   **loaf (about 1 pound) French bread, cut in half lengthwise**

3   **cups shredded iceberg lettuce**

24   **slices shaved smoked ham (about 7 ounces)**

24   **slices shaved smoked turkey breast (about 7 ounces)**

2   **medium tomatoes, thinly sliced**

8   **slices American cheese**

1   **green bell pepper, thinly sliced**

LET'S BEGIN Combine the salad dressing and Italian seasoning in a small bowl and stir to mix well. Spread the mixture evenly onto the cut sides of the bread.

FIX IT FAST Layer the remaining ingredients on the bottom half of the loaf and cover with the top half. To serve, cut the sandwich crosswise into 8 slices.

Makes 8 servings

Per serving: 340 calories, 19g protein, 37g carbohydrates, 13g fat, 5g saturated fat, 44mg cholesterol, 1,363mg sodium

Honey Couscous Salad

Prep **10 MINUTES**   *Cook* **5 MINUTES + STANDING**

- 1¼ cups water
- 1 cup couscous
- ¼ cup honey
- 2 tablespoons olive oil
- 2 teaspoons grated lemon zest
- ⅓ cup lemon juice
- ¼ teaspoon ground black pepper
- 1 teaspoon salt
- ½ pound cooked shredded chicken breast (about 2 cups)
- 1 can (15½ ounces) garbanzo beans, rinsed and drained
- 2 carrots, shredded
- 3 scallions, thinly sliced
- 3 tablespoons chopped parsley

Cut fixing time by using the food processor to shred the carrots and chop the parsley. However, shred chicken by hand, which takes only minutes. It's also good work for little helping hands.

LET'S BEGIN Bring the water to a boil in a medium saucepan. Remove from heat, stir in couscous, cover, and let stand 5 minutes. Fluff with a fork to separate the grains and transfer to a large bowl. Cool for 10 minutes. Meanwhile, combine the next 6 ingredients in a small bowl and set aside.

TOSS IT UP Add honey mixture and all the remaining ingredients to the couscous and toss to coat. Serve at room temperature or cover and refrigerate to serve later.

Makes 5 servings

Per serving: 410 calories, 24g protein, 60g carbohydrates, 8g fat, 1g saturated fat, 39mg cholesterol, 790mg sodium

RANCH-HAND ROASTED BEEF

Prep **10 MINUTES**

1	cup ranch-style salad dressing
8	teaspoons prepared horseradish
4	teaspoons chopped fresh parsley
4	teaspoons minced red bell pepper
12	ounces thinly sliced roast beef
4	kaiser rolls, split
8	slices red onion
8	slices tomato
2	cups shredded iceberg lettuce

Roast beef and horseradish are a classic combo for a reason: It's great! The tasty mix of ranch dressing and horseradish add punch to this sandwich. We've used red onion, but if you can find Vidalia, Walla Walla, or Texas Sweet onions in your market, use them instead.

LET'S BEGIN Combine the first 4 ingredients in a small bowl and stir to mix well.

LAYER & SERVE Divide the beef evenly on the bottoms of the rolls. Drizzle with the dressing mixture and stack with the onion, tomato, and lettuce. Cover with the tops of the rolls and serve immediately.

Makes 4 servings

Per serving: 592 calories, 24g protein, 40g carbohydrates, 38g fat, 6g saturated fat, 37mg cholesterol, 1,904mg sodium

PORK PO'-BOYS

Prep **15 MINUTES**

- 1 **loaf (1 pound) French or Italian bread**
- 1 **pound cooked boneless pork loin roast, thinly sliced**
- 1 **ripe tomato, thinly sliced**
- 1 **cucumber, thinly sliced**
- 1 **green bell pepper, thinly sliced**
- 1 **ripe avocado, peeled and sliced**
- 4 **ounces fresh spinach**
- 8 **ounces alfalfa sprouts**
- 4 **tablespoons Italian salad dressing**

Just like taking a trip to New Orleans! This fabulous sandwich was created there in the 1920s at the Martin Brothers Grocery. It can be filled with almost any meat you like. Sometimes fried oysters are the filling of choice. Create more color by adding yellow or red bell peppers. Take po'-boys along for picnics or tailgate parties. Serve with chips and your favorite beverages—or iced chicory coffee, like they do in the Big Easy.

FIX IT FAST Cut the bread in half lengthwise. Layer the bottom half with the next 7 ingredients and drizzle with the dressing. Cover with the top half and cut into slices to serve.

Makes 4 servings

Per serving: 720 calories, 49g protein, 72g carbohydrates, 27g fat, 6g saturated fat, 90mg cholesterol, 890mg sodium

SLOPPY JOE SUBS
Prep **10 MINUTES**   *Cook* **15 MINUTES**

1	pound 85% lean ground beef
1	teaspoon garlic salt
1	teaspoon dried Italian seasoning
¼	teaspoon ground black pepper
1	can (6 ounces) tomato paste
1½	cups water
1	package (1.31 ounces) Sloppy Joes seasoning mix
4	(6-inch) hoagie rolls, toasted
2	ounces shredded mozzarella cheese (½ cup)

The only thing that could possibly be better than a Sloppy Joe sandwich is a sub with even more of that great taste! Italian seasoning and Sloppy Joe seasoning mix guarantee it will taste just right, while the addition of shredded mozzarella adds just the right touch.

LET'S BEGIN Combine the beef, garlic salt, ¾ teaspoon of the Italian seasoning, and the pepper in a large bowl and stir to mix well. Shape into 16 (1½-inch) meatballs.

FLASH INTO THE PAN Brown the meatballs in a large skillet over medium-high heat for 10 minutes. Remove from the skillet and drain off the fat. Add the tomato paste, water, Sloppy Joes seasoning, and the remaining ¼ teaspoon Italian seasoning to the skillet and stir until mixture is smooth. Reduce the heat and simmer for 5 minutes.

STUFF & SERVE Place the meatballs in the rolls. Spoon the sauce over the meatballs and top with the mozzarella.

Makes 4 servings

Per serving: 405 calories, 30g protein, 33g carbohydrates, 17g fat, 7g saturated fat, 64mg cholesterol, 1,863mg sodium

GREEN BEAN & POTATO PARISIENNE

Prep **10 MINUTES**   *Cook* **14 MINUTES**

12	ounces small red potatoes, sliced ¼ inch thick
12	ounces green beans, trimmed
2	tablespoons olive oil
2	tablespoons white wine vinegar
1	tablespoon Dijon mustard
1	teaspoon garlic salt
½	teaspoon dried dill weed
½	teaspoon ground black pepper

To easily trim green beans, stack half a dozen or so, all facing the same way. Then with a large chef's knife, cut them with one whack!

LET'S BEGIN Place potatoes in a large saucepan and add enough water to cover by 2 inches. Cover the pan and bring to a boil over high heat. Reduce heat and simmer 2 to 3 minutes. Add green beans and continue to simmer 7 to 10 minutes, or until vegetables are tender.

TOSS IT UP Meanwhile, whisk together the remaining ingredients in a large bowl. Drain potatoes and beans, add to the bowl, and toss to coat. Serve immediately or cover and refrigerate to serve later.

Makes 6 servings

Per serving: 112 calories, 2g protein, 16g carbohydrates, 5g fat, 1g saturated fat, 0mg cholesterol, 470mg sodium

SPEEDY MEATBALL SANDWICHES

Prep **10 MINUTES**   *Cook* **11 MINUTES**

1	teaspoon vegetable oil
1	medium onion, cut into thin wedges (¾ cup)
1	medium green bell pepper, cut into thin strips (¾ cup)
12	ounces frozen fully cooked beef meatballs (about 23 meatballs)
1	jar (14 ounces) spaghetti sauce
4	hoagie rolls, split

Frozen cooked meatballs make this he-man sandwich a snap to prepare. For more cheesy flavor, sprinkle shredded Mozzarella over the meatballs and sauce.

LET'S BEGIN Heat the oil in large nonstick skillet over medium heat until hot. Add the onion and bell pepper and cook 5 minutes or until crisp-tender.

MAKE IT SAUCY Add the meatballs and the sauce and bring to a boil. Reduce the heat and simmer for 6 to 8 minutes or until the meatballs are heated through, stirring occasionally. Spoon the meatballs and sauce into the rolls.

Makes 4 servings

Per serving: 757 calories, 27g protein, 91g carbohydrates, 32g fat, 12g saturated fat, 55mg cholesterol, 1,760mg sodium

Speedy Meatball Sandwiches

SuperQuick

THAI TURKEY SANDWICHES

Prep **15 MINUTES**

Thai food doesn't get easier than this! Dried Thai seasoning is the secret! It's so filled with flavor that when mixed with cream cheese, it creates a sandwich spread with lots of oomph. Store-bought coleslaw speeds up this sandwich even more.

1	package (8 ounces) cream cheese, softened
3	teaspoons dried Thai seasoning
6	hoagie buns, toasted
1/3	cup Catalina or French salad dressing
4	cups shredded coleslaw mix
1/2	pound roasted sliced turkey
1/4	cup thinly sliced red onion

LET'S BEGIN Combine cream cheese and 1 teaspoon of the Thai seasoning in a small bowl and stir until mixed well. Spread evenly on both top and bottom portions of buns.

TOSS IT UP Combine the salad dressing and the remaining 2 teaspoons Thai seasoning in a large bowl and stir to mix well. Add coleslaw and toss to combine.

LAYER Arrange the turkey over the bottoms of the buns and top with coleslaw and onion.

Makes 6 servings

Per serving: 516 calories, 20g protein, 57g carbohydrates, 24g fat, 10g saturated fat, 57mg cholesterol, 1,382mg sodium

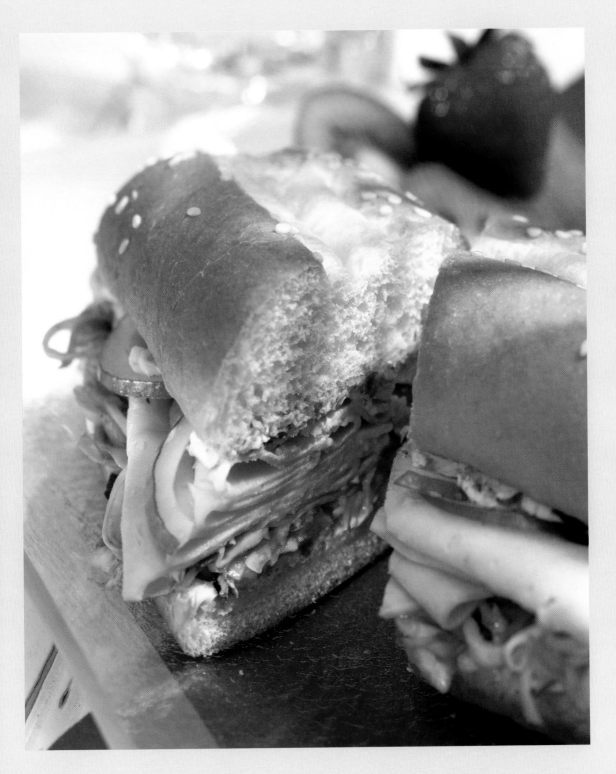

SuperQuick
PORK PITA POCKETS

Prep **15 MINUTES**   *Cook* **6 MINUTES**

2   tablespoons balsamic
    vinegar

1   tablespoon olive oil

½   teaspoon dried Italian
    seasoning

2   teaspoons red-pepper
    flakes

1   teaspoon fennel seed

8   thin boneless pork
    chops, about 1 pound

2   green bell peppers, each
    cut into 8 lengthwise
    strips

2   portobello mushrooms,
    each cut into 8 slices

1   large red onion, cut into
    8 wedges and separated
    into strips

4   pita pocket rounds, each
    cut in half

4   slices part-skim
    mozzarella cheese, cut in
    half

Pita sandwiches are fun to eat, and there is no chance of losing any of the tasty filling. These flavorful pockets are great for the lunch-box crowd, though if you prefer less-spicy food, reduce the amount of red-pepper flakes a bit.

LET'S BEGIN Preheat the broiler. Whisk together the first 5 ingredients in a small bowl. Coat a large baking pan with cooking spray. Brush the vinegar mixture on both sides of the pork chops. Arrange the pork, bell peppers, mushrooms, and onion in a single layer in the pan.

BROIL & STUFF Broil for 6 to 10 minutes, or until pork is browned and vegetables are crisp-tender, turning once. Divide the pork and vegetables among the pita pockets and top each with a piece of cheese.

Makes 4 servings
Per serving: 240 calories, 21g protein, 21g carbohydrates, 8g fat, 3g saturated fat, 75mg cholesterol, 280mg sodium

SZECHWAN SAUSAGE WRAPS

Prep **10 MINUTES**   *Cook* **16 MINUTES**

½ cup chopped walnuts

1 tablespoon vegetable oil

1 pound turkey sausage

2 to 3 teaspoons Szechwan seasoning

1 can (8 ounces) sliced water chestnuts, drained and chopped

1 cup shredded carrots

½ cup sliced scallions

3 tablespoons dry sherry or light soy sauce

8 large Bibb or leaf lettuce leaves

Tender leaf lettuce is a low-calorie and fun way to wrap a sandwich. Be sure to choose a lettuce with the largest leaves possible to hold all of the ingredients easily. Save time by using preshredded carrots.

LET'S BEGIN In a large skillet over medium heat, toast the walnuts, tossing occasionally, for 8 minutes, or until golden and fragrant. Set aside. Increase the heat to medium-high and add the oil. Add the sausage and the seasoning and cook for 6 minutes, or until cooked through, breaking up the sausage with a spoon.

BUBBLE & STIR Stir in the walnuts and the water chestnuts, carrots, scallions, and sherry. Cook, stirring constantly, for 2 to 3 minutes, or until heated through.

ROLL 'EM UP To serve, spoon about ½ cup of the sausage mixture into the center of each lettuce leaf, roll up, and tuck in the edges.

Makes 4 servings

Per serving: 446 calories, 26g protein, 18g carbohydrates, 30g fat, 7g saturated fat, 110mg cholesterol, 831mg sodium

MEDITERRANEAN STEAK SANDWICHES

Prep **5 MINUTES**   *Cook* **12 MINUTES**

1½   teaspoons dried basil

1½   teaspoons garlic powder

1½   teaspoons dried oregano

½   teaspoon salt

⅛   teaspoon ground black pepper

2   beef rib-eye steaks (about 1½ pounds), 1-inch thick

1   tablespoon olive oil

1   tablespoon lemon juice

4   pita pockets, warmed

2   tablespoons crumbled feta cheese

1   tablespoon chopped Kalamata or other black olives

A fast-to-fix blend of five herbs and spices flavors tender rib-eye steaks in this hearty one-dish meal. Eat this hefty sandwich with a knife and fork, so you don't miss a single delicious bite.

LET'S BEGIN Combine the first 5 ingredients in a small bowl and stir to mix well. Press mixture onto both sides of each of the steaks.

FLASH INTO THE PAN Heat the oil in a large nonstick skillet over medium heat until hot. Cook the steaks for 12 to 15 minutes for medium-rare to medium doneness, turning occasionally. Drizzle with the lemon juice. Cut the steaks into thin slices, place on top of pitas, and sprinkle with the cheese and olives.

Makes 4 servings

Per serving: 611 calories, 40g protein, 36g carbohydrates, 33g fat, 12g saturated fat, 92mg cholesterol, 769mg sodium

TERIYAKI TURKEY BURGERS

Prep **15 MINUTES**   *Cook* **15 MINUTES**

⅓   cup honey

¼   cup soy sauce

1½   teaspoons grated fresh ginger

1   teaspoon minced garlic

1   pound ground turkey

½   cup finely chopped celery

¼   cup thinly sliced scallions

4   hamburger buns, toasted

For the juiciest burgers, use ground turkey (a mix of white and dark meat) instead of turkey breast. Go easy when mixing the meat mixture or the burgers will be tough.

LET'S BEGIN Combine the first 4 ingredients in a small bowl and set aside.

SEASON AND SHAPE Stir turkey, celery, scallions, and 3 tablespoons of the honey mixture in a large bowl. Shape into 4 patties, ½ to ¾ inch thick.

FIRE UP THE GRILL Cook the burgers over hot coals, brushing with the remaining honey mixture and turning often, for about 15 minutes, or until well browned and cooked through. Serve burgers on toasted buns.

Makes 4 servings

Per serving: 397 calories, 25g protein, 48g carbohydrates, 12g fat, 3g saturated fat, 90mg cholesterol, 1,401mg sodium

SOUTHWESTERN ROLL-UPS

Prep **10 MINUTES+ CHILLING**

¼ cup salad dressing or mayonnaise

½ cup chunky salsa

4 (10-inch) flour tortillas

2 ounces thinly sliced smoked turkey or roast beef

2 ounces shredded Cheddar cheese (½ cup)

1 cup shredded iceberg lettuce

Turn these into hot roll-ups 1, 2, 3. Omit the lettuce, wrap each roll-up in a paper towel, and microwave separately on High for 1 minute, or until heated through.

LET'S BEGIN Combine the salad dressing and the salsa in a small bowl and stir to mix well.

LAYER & ROLL Spread the salad dressing mixture evenly onto one side of each tortilla. Top with the meat, cheese, and lettuce and roll up. Wrap each roll-up in plastic wrap and refrigerate for 1 hour to allow flavors to blend.

Makes 4 servings

Per serving: 317 calories, 11g protein, 26g carbohydrates, 19g fat, 5g saturated fat, 31mg cholesterol, 744mg sodium

BERRY TURKEY BAGEL

Prep **15 MINUTES + CHILLING**

½ cup finely chopped celery

½ cup finely chopped dried cranberries, dried cherries, or raisins

⅓ cup mayonnaise

1 tablespoon Dijon mustard

4 bagels, split

8 ounces thinly sliced deli turkey breast

4 slices American cheese

4 lettuce leaves

Thanks to dried cranberries, you can enjoy this fruit year-round, not just when the fresh berries are in the market. Here they are used to flavor mayonnaise for the turkey-and-American cheese sandwiches. The dried berries are great to toss into muffins, cookies, and quick breads, too.

LET'S BEGIN Stir the celery, cranberries, mayonnaise, and mustard together in a small bowl. Cover and refrigerate for at least 1 hour.

LAYER To assemble the sandwiches, spread the cranberry mixture over both halves of the bagels. Layer each bottom half with turkey, cheese, and lettuce, then cover with the bagel tops.

Makes 4 servings

Per serving: 460 calories, 25g protein, 58g carbohydrates, 14g fat, 5g saturated fat, 45mg cholesterol, 1,690mg sodium

Berry Turkey Bagel

Autumn Beef Stew, page 88

All in One Pot

Here's what traditional one-dish cooking is really all about. Toss together a fast pasta, stir a slow-cookin' chowder, or mix a pot of chili the fast and easy way. Unlike the soups and stews of grandma's day, ours take a few shortcuts to cut preparation and cleanup time without sacrificing the taste. Use a ready-made pot roast in the Autumn Beef Stew and serve it up in less than half an hour, or use a mix to stir up a mac 'n' cheese dish in just 15 minutes. But that's not all. Discover the best pastas and onions to throw into the pot, fun ways to top a stew, and flavorful ways to create sauces that taste truly homemade. Now, get out your pot and start cookin'!

LEMON DILL SALMON WITH RED POTATOES

Prep **10 MINUTES**   *Cook* **27 MINUTES**

1   **pound new red potatoes, cut into 1-inch pieces (4 cups)**

¾   **cup water**

1   **pound salmon fillet**

¼   **cup white wine or apple juice**

1   **tablespoon chopped fresh dill or 1 teaspoon dried**

1½   **cups fresh pea pods, trimmed**

2   **tablespoons lemon juice**

1   **teaspoon cornstarch**

¼   **teaspoon salt**

The rich taste of salmon makes it the perfect partner for tender potatoes and fresh dill.

LET'S BEGIN Place the potatoes in a large skillet, add the water, and bring to a boil. Reduce the heat to low, cover, and simmer for 10 minutes. Lay the salmon fillet on top of the potatoes. Sprinkle with the wine and dill.

SIMMER LOW Simmer, covered, for 10 to 12 minutes, or until the fish flakes with a fork. Add the peas, cover, and simmer for an additional 2 to 4 minutes, or until tender. Remove the skin from the salmon and break the fish into bite-size chunks.

MAKE IT SAUCY Mix the lemon juice and cornstarch, then carefully stir into the salmon mixture. Increase the heat to medium-high and bring to a boil. Season with the salt.

Makes 4 servings

Per serving: 290 calories, 27g protein, 26g carbohydrates, 7g fat, 2g saturated fat, 60mg cholesterol, 200mg sodium

ASPARAGUS, SHRIMP & ANGEL HAIR

Prep **20 MINUTES**   *Cook* **8 MINUTES**

8   ounces angel hair pasta

1   package (10 ounces) frozen asparagus cuts

⅓   cup chicken broth

2   teaspoons olive oil

2   garlic cloves, minced

2   tablespoons dried basil

¼   teaspoon salt

Pinch ground black pepper

8   ounces medium cooked and peeled shrimp

2   tomatoes, seeded and chopped

½   cup sliced scallions

¼   cup grated Parmesan cheese

This dish tastes just like spring! To cut down on some of your kitchen time, buy precooked shrimp. It's worth the extra cost.

LET'S BEGIN Cook the pasta according to package directions. Drain and rinse the pasta under cold water to cool, and drain again. Meanwhile, cook the asparagus according to package directions, drain and plunge into ice water to stop the cooking process, Then drain again.

TOSS IT UP Whisk together the next 6 ingredients in a large mixing bowl. Add the pasta, asparagus and remaining ingredients and toss the salad gently with the dressing. Serve immediately or cover and refrigerate for several hours, if you wish, before serving.

Makes 4 servings
Per serving: 370 calories, 28g protein, 50g carbohydrates, 6g fat, 1g saturated fat, 115mg cholesterol, 404mg sodium

---

Time Savers

HERE'S DINNER, WHEN THERE'S NO TIME TO COOK

On those days when you don't have time to cook, you can still serve great meals in minutes, thanks to the fully cooked, ready-to-heat products in your grocer's refrigerated case. Here are some of the great one-dish helpers we found to get supper off to a fast start.

• **CHICKEN FOR SUPPER.** There's a whole array of heat 'n' eat chicken items in your grocer's refrigerated case: whole, fully roasted birds for 2 or more or roasted chicken breasts—original recipe, honey roasted, or grilled Italian; mesquite-grilled chicken breast fillets in a bag; and breaded and fried chicken nuggets for the kindergarten crowd.

• **PORK BARBECUE.** Throw a large rack of ribs, already fully cooked, on the barbecue for an instant party.

• **BEEF TO GO.** Thanks to your microwave, you can serve roast beef within a minute's notice: pot roast in a rich gravy; sliced roast of beef au jus; country fried steak; home-style meatballs; seasoned beef strips perfect for a stir-fry.

SLOW COOKIN' CORN CHOWDER

Prep **20 MINUTES**   *Cook* **8 TO 9 HOURS**

6   slices bacon, cooked until crisp, chopped

1½   pounds red potatoes, peeled and cubed (5 cups)

1   bag (16 ounces) frozen whole kernel corn

¼   cup dehydrated minced onion

2   cans (14½ ounces each) chicken broth

1   cup water

2   teaspoons garlic salt

¼   teaspoon turmeric

1   teaspoon ground black pepper

1   can (12 ounces) evaporated milk

8   ounces shredded Monterey Jack or white Cheddar cheese (2 cups)

Dried chopped chives (optional)

A hearty bowl of chowder is always a welcome sight at dinnertime. Here the combination of bacon, potatoes, corn, and Jack cheese makes the best chowder ever. Serve with warm sourdough and a green salad. In a hurry? Skip the slow cooker, and make this chowder on the stovetop in 25 minutes.

LET'S BEGIN Combine all ingredients except the milk, cheese, and chives in a slow cooker and stir to mix well. Cover and cook on high for 8 to 9 hours, or until potatoes are tender.

MAKE IT CHEESY Add milk and cheese and stir to combine. Cover and heat 2 to 3 minutes or until cheese melts. Garnish each serving with chives, if you like.

STOVE-TOP CORN CHOWDER

Combine all ingredients except the milk, cheese, and chives in a large pot. Cover and bring to a boil over high heat. Reduce heat and simmer 20 minutes or until potatoes are tender, adding an additional 1 cup of broth if chowder becomes too thick. Add milk and cheese and cook, stirring constantly, 5 minutes or until cheese melts. Garnish each serve with chives, if you like.

Makes 10 servings

Per serving: 271 calories, 12g protein, 30g carbohydrates, 12g fat, 6g saturated fat, 38mg cholesterol, 1,081mg sodium

HERB 'TATER POT

Prep **10 MINUTES** *Cook* **15 MINUTES**

2   cups frozen southern-style hash brown potatoes

1½ cups frozen sliced carrots

2   tablespoons dehydrated minced onion

1   can (14½ ounces) chicken or vegetable broth

1   cup water

Herb & Spice Blend (see recipe)

1   cup light cream

2   tablespoons butter or margarine

Mix a double or triple batch of the herb-and-spice blend. The mix of coriander, basil, celery flakes, garlic salt, cayenne, and black pepper can be used to flavor lots of other soups, too.

LET'S BEGIN Combine all ingredients except cream and butter in a large saucepan. Cover and bring to a boil, reduce heat, and simmer 5 minutes, or until potatoes and carrots are tender.

SIMMER & SERVE Add cream and butter, simmer to heat through, and serve immediately.

HERB & SPICE BLEND

Combine in a small bowl: ½ teaspoon dried basil, ½ teaspoon dried celery flakes, ½ teaspoon garlic salt, ¼ teaspoon ground coriander, ¼ teaspoon ground black pepper, and ⅛ teaspoon cayenne pepper. Mix to blend well.

Makes 5 servings

Per serving: 281 calories, 4g protein, 22g carbohydrates, 20g fat, 13g saturated fat, 65mg cholesterol, 684mg sodium

---

Time Savers

TWO DINNERS FROM ONE POT

When you have some cooking time on the weekends, stir up one of our one-pot meals. Consider doubling the recipe so you'll have enough for two meals. Here are some ways two of our recipes do "double duty":

Slow Cookin' Corn Chowder (opposite page). After enjoying big bowls of chowder one day, turn the rest of the pot into a chicken corn stew. Just add strips of boneless, skinless grilled chicken breasts, and some blanched baby carrots. The original recipe makes 10 servings, so that might be plenty. The recipe doubles just fine.

Herb 'Tater Pot (above). Double the recipe so there will be plenty left to make a Ham & 'Tater Stew the next day. Add cubed ham and a little fresh snipped dill, and top it off with some shredded Cheddar.

Ham 'n' Cheese Pasta

Prep **25 MINUTES**   *Cook* **16 MINUTES**

12   ounces rotini

1   can (14½ ounces) diced tomatoes with garlic and onion

Milk

2   tablespoons butter

3   tablespoons all-purpose flour

1   teaspoon dried basil, crushed

2   cups shredded sharp Cheddar cheese

1½   cups diced cooked ham

Salt and ground black pepper

Chopped fresh parsley (optional)

We love the spiral shape of rotini (it easily holds all the tasty sauce), but any favorite tube shape will also work well.

LET'S BEGIN Cook pasta according to package directions. Drain and set aside. Drain the tomatoes and reserve the liquid. Add enough milk to the tomato liquid to measure 2 cups.

MAKE IT SAUCY Melt the butter in the pasta pot over medium heat. Stir in the flour and basil and cook for 3 minutes, stirring constantly. Add the reserved milk mixture and cook for 3 minutes, or until thickened, stirring constantly.

STIR & HEAT Stir in the reserved tomatoes, pasta, cheese and ham and cook 3 minutes or until heated through. Season to taste with salt and pepper and garnish with parsley, if you wish.

Makes 4 servings

Per serving: 744 calories, 39g protein, 77g carbohydrates, 31g fat, 17g saturated fat, 106mg cholesterol, 1,706mg sodium

Cooking Basics

PASTAS PERFECT FOR THE POT!

Everyone loves a cozy one-pot meal of pasta. It's the ultimate comfort food! Whether it's a soup, a stew, or a casserole, pasta is perfect for any pot. And there are many to choose from: big chunky tubes, tiny grains, and long, delicate strands. Choosing and using the right pasta is no work at all!

PREPARE IT AHEAD Cook up the pasta in a separate pot or make it ahead. Drain well—but don't rinse

it. Toss it into a resealable plastic bag and set refrigerate up to several hours. Microwave before serving just long enough to heat it through.

COOK IT TOGETHER For soups and stews, small pastas—such as orzo, pastina, tubetti, and elbows—are great. They don't take long to cook, so add them to the stew or soup pot about 20 minutes before the cooking is done. Pastas will continue to absorb liquid as it rests.

PICK IT RIGHT For hearty, robust dishes, choose pastas that hold their shape well, such as rigatoni, ziti, and wagon wheels. Choose stars and other tiny shapes for lighter dishes and soups. For casseroles, reach for bow ties, shells, and penne pasta. And for meatball and tomato type dishes, use a heavier strand pasta, such as bucatini or fettuccine. Stir them right in—they won't break apart!

WESTERN WAGON WHEELS

Prep **5 MINUTES**   *Cook* **21 MINUTES**

1	pound 85% lean ground beef
1	can (14½ ounces) stewed tomatoes
1	package (10 ounces) frozen corn
4	ounces wagon wheel pasta
½	cup barbecue sauce
1½	cups water
Salt and ground black pepper	

Cook up this gem for the little cowboys and cowgirls in your family. Barbecue sauce makes it real flavorful, without much fuss from you. And the wagon wheel pasta can't be beat for eating fun.

LET'S BEGIN Cook the beef in a large skillet over medium heat for 6 minutes or until beef is brown, breaking it up with a spoon. Add next five ingredients and bring to a boil.

SIMMER LOW Reduce the heat to low, cover and simmer 15 to 20 minutes or until pasta is tender, stirring occasionally. Stir in salt and pepper to taste.

Makes 4 servings

Per serving: 581 calories, 40g protein, 65g carbohydrates, 18g fat, 7g saturated fat, 75mg cholesterol, 637mg sodium

CHICKEN BROCCOLI MAC

Prep **5 MINUTES**   *Cook* **10 MINUTES**

1	package (7¼ ounces) macaroni and cheese dinner
1	cup cooked broccoli florets
1	cup chopped cooked chicken
½	cup salad dressing
2	teaspoons Dijon mustard

Everybody loves macaroni and cheese! Make it even better by adding good-for-you broccoli, chicken chunks, and salad dressing. Pick a mild and creamy dressing for the best flavor.

FIX IT FAST Prepare the macaroni and cheese dinner according to package directions.

HEAT & SERVE Add the remaining ingredients and cook for 3 minutes over low heat or until heated through, stirring occasionally.

Makes 4 servings

Per serving: 355 calories, 18g protein, 31g carbohydrates, 18g fat, 4g saturated fat, 47mg cholesterol, 718mg sodium

PIEROGIES PESTO

Prep **10 MINUTES**   *Cook* **12 MINUTES**

1   package (16.9 ounces) potato and onion or potato and Cheddar pierogies (frozen)

1   pound asparagus, trimmed and cut into 1-inch pieces

½   cup prepared pesto sauce

4   ounces smoked ham, cut in ¼-inch strips

2   tablespoons toasted pine nuts

Chopped fresh basil (optional)

Little Polish dumplings, known as pierogies, are the ultimate comfort food. Both the potato-onion and potato-Cheddar varieties will be super with the pesto sauce, ham, and asparagus. If you don't have pine nuts, walnuts will do just fine.

LET'S BEGIN Cook pierogies according to package directions, adding asparagus during the last two minutes of cooking. Drain, reserving ¼ cup of the cooking water. Set the pierogies and asparagus aside and keep warm.

HEAT AND TOSS Combine pesto sauce, ham and reserved cooking water in the same pot and cook over medium heat 5 minutes, or until heated though. Add the pierogies and toss to coat. Garnish with the pine nuts and fresh basil, if you wish.

Makes 3 servings

Per serving: 574 calories, 26g protein, 61g carbohydrates, 26g fat, 7g saturated fat, 47mg cholesterol, 1,597mg sodium

AUTUMN BEEF STEW

Prep **10 MINUTES**   *Cook* **11 MINUTES**

1   package (1¾ to 2½ pounds) fully cooked boneless beef pot roast with gravy

1   pound small mushrooms

2   small onions, cut into thin wedges

⅔   cup dry red wine

¾   teaspoon dried marjoram

1   tablespoon cornstarch

3   tablespoons water

Hot cooked egg noodles

Red wine, mushrooms, and a bit of marjoram add just the right homey touch to this almost-instant, hearty one-dish meal.

LET'S BEGIN Remove the roast from the package and transfer the gravy to a Dutch oven. Add the mushrooms, onions, wine, and marjoram and bring to a boil. Reduce the heat to medium-low and cook for 7 to 8 minutes, or until the vegetables are almost tender, stirring occasionally.

BUBBLE & STIR Meanwhile, combine the cornstarch and water in a small bowl, stir until well mixed, and set aside. Cut the roast into 1-inch pieces, add to the pot, and cook for 3 minutes, or until heated through. Stir in the cornstarch mixture, increase heat to medium, bring to a boil, and cook for 1 minute, stirring constantly until thickened and bubbly. Serve the stew over the noodles.

Makes 4 servings

Per serving: 710 calories, 54g protein, 43g carbohydrates, 33g fat, 12g saturated fat, 157mg cholesterol, 250mg sodium

Cooking Basics

PICKING THE ONION FOR THE POT

Storage onions are the ever-familiar onions with brown, papery skin. There are several varieties of these.

• **Spanish onions** are large and sweet and are perfect for all types of cooking, especially the soup pot and stew pot.

• **Yellow onions** have a medium to strong flavor. They can be used raw or cooked and are the onion to use any time at all.

• **White onions,** with their sharp flavor and strong bite, are the most pungent. Use them when you want more onion flavor, raw or cooked.

• **Red onions** are beloved for their color and are most often used raw.

• **Shallots** are crisp and refined with a delicate onion flavor. They are especially great roasted and pan-fried.

    Fresh onions have low sulfur content so they won't bring tears to your eyes!

• **Scallions and spring onions** have a crisp, clean taste makes them ideal in salads and stir-fries.

• **Leeks** have a delicate onion flavor and are great in soups and stews. Just be sure to rinse them well to remove all their grit.

• **Vidalia, Maui, and Walla Walla onions** are so sweet they can be eaten out of hand. Look for them in spring. Use to top off burgers or toss into salads.

FAST & EASY BEEF CHILI POT

Prep **5 MINUTES**   *Cook* **16 MINUTES + STANDING**

1   pound 85% lean ground beef

1   can (15 ounces) chili hot beans in chili sauce, undrained

1   can (14½ ounces) chili-style diced tomatoes

1   cup frozen corn

¼   teaspoon ground black pepper

Shredded Mexican cheese blend or Cheddar cheese

Sour cream

Everything about this recipe says FAST: the ingredients, the short prep, and the cooking time. This is just the meal to serve on those weeknights when you need to put a good meal on the table but you're short on energy.

LET'S BEGIN Brown beef in a medium nonstick skillet over medium heat for 6 minutes. Combine with the next 4 ingredients in a 2-quart microwave-safe dish and stir to mix well. Cover and microwave on High for 6 minutes. Stir the chili and microwave for 4 to 6 more minutes, or until heated through.

LET IT REST Remove chili from the microwave and let it stand for 3 minutes, covered. Top each serving with cheese and sour cream.

Makes 4 servings

Per serving: 367 calories, 28g protein, 33g carbohydrates, 15g fat, 6g saturated fat, 60mg cholesterol, 1,323mg sodium

SHRIMP CREOLE STEW

Prep **5 MINUTES**   *Cook* **20 MINUTES**

Jumbo-size bags of ready-to-cook shrimp are available in the food warehouse stores that have become so popular. And the price is right, too! Keep a bag in your freezer for an on-the-spot shrimp cocktail or this impromptu Creole stew for unexpected guests.

6	ounces small peeled shrimp (1½ cups)
1	bag (16 ounces) frozen broccoli, cauliflower and red pepper blend
1	can (14½ ounces) diced tomatoes
1	teaspoon vegetable oil
1	to 2 teaspoons hot sauce
1½	teaspoons salt
3	cups hot cooked Spanish or white rice

FIX IT FAST Combine all ingredients except cooked rice in a large saucepan, cover and bring to a boil.

SIMMER LOW Reduce heat to medium-low and simmer for 20 minutes. Serve over rice.

Makes 4 servings

Per serving (includes ¾ cup cooked Spanish rice):
324 calories, 24g protein, 44g carbohydrates, 6g fat, 1g saturated fat, 129mg cholesterol, 1,941mg sodium

Cook to Cook

HOW DO YOU TOP OFF A SIMPLE STEW?

❝I have found that a hearty stew lends itself to all kinds of tasty toppings. I often ladle portions of beef stew into deep soup bowls (the ones that go into the oven). And then *I pipe a thick border of mashed potatoes all around the edge and sprinkle a little paprika on each one.* Or you can transfer the stew to a casserole or baking dish, cover the stew with mashed potatoes, and top with a generous layer of shredded Cheddar. Then I pop it under the broiler for a minute or two, just long enough to melt the cheese.

It's also fun to top chicken stew with fresh-baked buttermilk biscuits.

When I make a tender veal stew, *I spoon a generous dollop of prepared pesto over each serving.*

Don't forget about Gremolata. That's the flavor-packed mix of chopped garlic, parsley, and grated lemon zest that adds pizzazz to almost any favorite stew. And, of course, *a handful of coarsely chopped mixed herbs adds that casual elegance to any stew pot.*❞

SuperQuick
SHRIMP GUMBO

Prep **15 MINUTES**   Cook **14 MINUTES**

We love versatile pierogies because they can be combined with so many different ingredients for delicious, easy dinners. Here they take on the flavors of Louisiana. Cut down on the chopping and cleaning by picking up already-sliced red bell peppers and already-peeled and cleaned shrimp.

2	tablespoons olive oil
1	large onion, thinly sliced
2	red bell peppers, cut into thin strips
1	tablespoon minced garlic
¼	teaspoon red pepper flakes
1	can (14 ounces) low-sodium chicken broth
1	package (16.9 ounces) potato and Cheddar cheese pierogies (frozen)
1	pound large shrimp, peeled and deveined
1	bay leaf

Chopped fresh parsley (optional)

LET'S BEGIN Heat the oil in a large deep skillet over medium-high heat. Add the onion and peppers. Cover and cook for 4 minutes. Uncover and cook about 3 minutes, stirring occasionally, until vegetables are lightly browned. Add garlic and pepper flakes and cook for 30 seconds, stirring.

BUBBLE & STIR Add the broth and bring to a boil. Add the pierogies, cover, and cook for 3 minutes. Add shrimp and bay leaf. Cover and cook 3 minutes longer, stirring once, until shrimp are cooked.

SERVE Remove the bay leaf. Spoon into soup bowls and sprinkle each serving with chopped parsley, if you wish.

Makes 4 servings

Per serving: 381 calories, 28g protein, 43g carbohydrates, 11g fat, 3g saturated fat, 151mg cholesterol, 724mg sodium

---

On the Menu

Enjoy the best of the Big Easy with this Cajun-style menu. As the locals in New Orleans say, "Bon temp rouler!" (Let the good times roll!)

Peppery Cheese Straws

Iceberg and Garden Tomato Salad with Thousand Island Dressing

Shrimp Gumbo

Skillet Cornbread

Pecan Pie with Bourbon Whipped Cream

ZESTY CHICKEN & VEGETABLE SOUP

Prep **5 MINUTES** *Cook* **10 MINUTES**

8 ounces boneless, skinless chicken breast, cut into very thin strips

1 tablespoon hot-pepper sauce

4 cups chicken broth

1 package (16 ounces) frozen stir-fry vegetables

1 cup angel hair pasta, broken into 2-inch lengths, or fine egg noodles

1 green onion, thinly sliced

Cook up a double batch of this almost-instant satisfying soup that's chock full of chicken and vegetables. Freeze what you don't use in small freeze-safe airtight containers for up to several months. Bring it out some wintry eve. For a little crunch, top the soup with canned french-fried onion rings right before serving.

LET'S BEGIN Toss the chicken with the pepper sauce and set aside. Bring the broth to a boil in a large saucepan over medium-high heat.

INTO THE PAN Add the vegetables and pasta to the broth. Return to a boil and cook for 2 minutes. Stir in the chicken and green onion. Cook for 1 minute, or until the chicken is no longer pink.

Makes 4 servings

Per serving: 165 calories, 21g protein, 12g carbohydrates, 3g fat, 1g saturated fat, 42mg cholesterol, 852mg sodium

---

Microwave in Minutes

SPEEDING UP THE POT

Your microwave is a treasured tool when it comes to making that one-pot recipe cook faster. The secret? Precook some of the ingredients in the microwave so they'll already be cooking by the time they're added to the pot. Here are some ingredients that work well:

• **Potatoes.** Partial cook on High in the microwave. Wrap them in a kitchen towel and let stand for

5 minutes, then peel if you wish and add to the stew pot.

• **Carrots and green beans.** Spread out into a single layer in a microwaveable pie plate. Sprinkle with water, cover with plastic wrap, and vent a corner. Cook on High just until the vegetables start to cook. Add to the stew pot the last 15 minutes of cooking.

• **Bacon.** Cook between paper towels until bacon becomes

translucent and begins to crisp slightly. Let rest in the paper towel a couple of minutes, then cut into slivers and add to the stew pot the last few minutes of cooking.

• **Rice.** Use either instant rice that cooks in 5 minutes or packets of ready-to-heat rice that cook in 90 seconds. Follow the directions for microwaving, then toss into the pot the last few minutes of cooking.

GREEN BEAN & TURKEY BAKE

Prep **25 MINUTES**   *Cook* **48 MINUTES**

1   can (10¾ ounces) cream of mushroom soup

¾   cup milk

⅛   teaspoon ground black pepper

2   packages (9 ounces each) frozen cut green beans, thawed, or 2 cans (14½ ounces each) cut green beans, drained

12   ounces cubed cooked turkey or chicken (2 cups)

1⅓   cups french-fried onions

6   ounces shredded Cheddar cheese(1½ cups)

Hot cooked mashed potatoes

This is a great prep-ahead meal. Put the casserole together early in the day and refrigerate. Then simply pop it into the oven until nice and bubbly—dinner's ready!

LET'S BEGIN Preheat the oven to 375°F. Whisk the soup, milk, and pepper together in a 3-quart casserole. Stir in the beans, turkey, ⅔ cup of the onions, and 1 cup of the cheese. Spoon 3 cups mashed potatoes or 6 servings instant mashed potatoes, cooked according to package directions, over the top.

INTO THE OVEN Bake, uncovered, for 45 minutes, or until hot. Sprinkle with the remaining ½ cup cheese and ⅔ cup onions. Bake for 3 minutes, or until the onions are golden brown.

Makes 6 servings

Per serving: 490 calories, 28g protein, 34g carbohydrates, 26g fat, 11g saturated fat, 78mg cholesterol, 1,047mg sodium

---

Microwave in Minutes

FAST-COOK IN THE MICROWAVE

Prepare recipe in the baking dish as above, but don't top with the mashed potatoes. Cover the dish with vented plastic wrap. Microwave on High for 15 minutes or until heated through, stirring once after 8 minutes. Remove the plastic wrap, spoon the mashed potatoes on top and sprinkle with the rest of the cheese and onions. Microwave on High for 2 to 4 minutes. Let stand for 5 minutes.

Asian Beef & Noodles, page 104

Global Fare

Pack your bags and come with us to faraway places, where simple one-dish dinners let you try new flavors. Start off in Italy with a slice of their favorite lasagna, made the no-fuss way. Hop over to France for some chicken in white wine sauce, then it's off to Russia for a stroganoff, made the time-saving way. And don't forget to stop in the Orient for chicken lo mein, made easier than ever with precut fresh vegetables. Back in America, take a boat ride on the bayous in Cajun country and feast on a traditional paella cooked up by the Spanish locals. Then drive over to Tex-Mex land to discover the many ways to serve dinner by rolling, folding, and stuffing a tortilla. Olé!

No-Fuss Beef Lasagna

Prep **10 MINUTES**   *Bake* **51 MINUTES + STANDING**

1   **pound 85% lean ground beef**

1   **jar (26 to 30 ounces) spaghetti sauce**

1   **can (14½ ounces) Italian-style diced tomatoes**

¼   **teaspoon cayenne pepper**

¼   **teaspoon salt**

1   **container (15 ounces) ricotta cheese**

¼   **cup grated Parmesan cheese**

1   **egg, lightly beaten**

10   **uncooked lasagna noodles**

1½   **cups shredded mozzarella cheese (6 ounces)**

Lots of meaty tomato sauce makes this layered noodle dish hearty and filling. And by using no-cook noodles you have one less pot to clean. If you're watching calories, use part-skim ricotta and mozzarella cheese.

LET'S BEGIN Preheat the oven to 375°F. Cook the beef in a large nonstick skillet over medium heat for 8 to 10 minutes, or until no longer pink, breaking it up with a spoon. Drain off any fat. Stir in the next 4 ingredients.

LAYER Combine the ricotta, Parmesan, and egg in a medium bowl and stir to mix well. Spread 2 cups of the beef sauce in the bottom of a 13 × 9-inch baking dish. Top with 4 of the noodles, arranged lengthwise in a single layer. Place a fifth noodle crosswise at the end of the dish, breaking the noodle to fit. Press the noodles lightly into the sauce. Spread all the ricotta mixture over the noodles. Sprinkle ricotta with 1 cup of the mozzarella and top with 1½ cups of the beef sauce. Top with the remaining noodles in a single layer, pressing noodles into the sauce. Top the noodles with the remaining beef sauce.

INTO THE OVEN Bake the lasagna for 45 minutes, or until the noodles are tender. Sprinkle with the remaining ½ cup mozzarella and let stand for 15 minutes for easier cutting.

Makes 9 servings

Per serving: 422 calories, 26g protein, 32g carbohydrates, 24g fat, 12g saturated fat, 99mg cholesterol, 938mg sodium

BEEF & NOODLES STROGANOFF

Prep **15 MINUTES**   *Cook* **12 MINUTES**

Stroganoff is made super-easy by using lean ground beef instead of sliced. Serve over hot wide egg noodles—they're perfect for sopping up all of the fabulous sauce flavors. Save time by using packaged sliced mushrooms. Be Hungarian—finish off with apple strudel.

1	pound 85% lean ground beef
1	medium onion, chopped (½ cup)
4	ounces sliced fresh mushrooms (1 cup)
1	cup sour cream
¾	cup cottage cheese
1	teaspoon salt
½	teaspoon ground black pepper
¼	teaspoon ground nutmeg
4	cups cooked extra-wide egg noodles (8 ounces dried)

Chopped fresh parsley

LET'S BEGIN Cook the ground beef, onion, and mushrooms in a large skillet over medium heat for 9 to 11 minutes, or until the beef is browned. Stir in the sour cream, cottage cheese, and seasonings. Simmer, stirring, for 3 to 5 minutes, or until hot and bubbly.

SERVE IT UP Spoon the beef mixture over the hot noodles and sprinkle with the parsley.

Makes 8 servings

Per serving: 300 calories, 18g protein, 25g carbohydrates, 14g fat, 7g saturated fat, 80mg cholesterol, 410mg sodium

Food Facts

STROGANOFF— THE ROYAL CONNECTION

Toward the end of the 19th century, Count Paul Stroganoff, a member of the court of Tsar Alexander III lived a life of the royals in St. Petersburg. Though little else is known about him, we do know he loved dining well and enjoying life to its fullest.

In spite of his unknown accomplishments, his name is now a legend. As the tale goes, his name became linked to several dishes made with beef, veal, pork, or game—all of them made even richer with an abundance of sour cream. Many variations exist, but they often have a spicy bite of mustard in them. Though Count Stroganoff's other achievements are little known, the elegant dish with his same name is famous.

FETTUCCINE PRIMAVERA
Prep **15 MINUTES**   *Cook* **15 MINUTES**

1	package (9 ounces) refrigerated fettuccine
¾	cup water
1	cup broccoli florets
½	cup each sliced carrots and red bell pepper strips
3	tablespoons butter or margarine
2	tablespoons all-purpose flour
1	cup evaporated milk
½	cup chicken broth
2	ounces shredded Parmesan cheese (½ cup)
2	ounces shredded provolone cheese (½ cup)
⅛	teaspoon cayenne pepper

Ground black pepper

Parmesan and provolone cheese make this popular pasta dish even better. You can use other vegetables (choose colorful ones!).

LET'S BEGIN Cook the pasta according to package directions and keep warm. Bring the water to a boil in a medium saucepan and add the broccoli, carrots, and red pepper. Reduce the heat and simmer for 5 to 7 minutes, or until the vegetables are tender. Drain and keep warm.

MAKE IT SAUCY Melt the butter in the same saucepan over medium heat, stir in the flour, and cook for 1 minute, stirring constantly. Gradually stir in the milk and chicken broth and cook for 5 minutes, stirring constantly, until the mixture boils and thickens. Add the Parmesan, provolone, cayenne, and black pepper to taste. Stir until the cheese melts.

TOSS IT UP Transfer the pasta, vegetables, and milk mixture to a large serving bowl and toss to coat.

Makes 4 servings

Per serving: 514 calories, 19g protein, 52g carbohydrates, 22g fat, 13g saturated fat, 51mg cholesterol, 535mg sodium

CHICKEN LO MEIN

Prep **15 MINUTES + MARINATING**   *Cook* **15 MINUTES**

2   boneless, skinless chicken breast halves, cut into thin strips

1   tablespoon + ⅓ cup stir-fry sauce

¼   pound capellini (angel hair pasta)

3   tablespoons water

2   tablespoons vegetable oil

¼   pound fresh snow peas, cut into matchsticks

1   large carrot, cut into matchsticks

⅛   teaspoon salt

2   teaspoons toasted sesame seeds

Lo mein is one of those really versatile dishes that can be whipped up with almost any favorite combination of vegetables. If you like, you can also use strips of pork or peeled and deveined shrimp—or use a mix. Save time by using precut matchstick carrots. Then turn what you don't use into carrot–raisin slaw.

LET'S BEGIN Place the chicken and 1 tablespoon of the stir-fry sauce in a resealable plastic bag. Press out the air and marinate in the refrigerator for 30 minutes. Meanwhile, cook the pasta according to package directions, omitting the salt. Drain, rinse under cold running water, and drain again. Combine the remaining ⅓ cup stir-fry sauce and the water in a small bowl, stir to mix well, and set aside.

STIR-FRY Heat 1 tablespoon of the oil in a wok or large skillet over high heat. Add the chicken and stir-fry for 2 minutes or until no longer pink. Remove the chicken from the wok. Add the remaining oil to the pan, then add the peas, carrots, and salt and stir-fry 4 minutes, or until vegetables are crisp-tender.

TOSS IT UP Add the reserved sauce mixture, chicken, pasta, and sesame seeds and cook 3 minutes, stirring constantly, until all ingredients are coated with sauce and the pasta is heated through.

Makes 4 servings

Per serving: 290 calories, 19g protein, 32g carbohydrates, 9g fat, 1g saturated fat, 34mg cholesterol, 942mg sodium

COQ AU VIN BLANC

Prep **15 MINUTES**   *Cook/Bake* **56 MINUTES**

½   cup all-purpose flour

½   teaspoon salt

¼   teaspoon ground black pepper

1   whole chicken (4 pounds), cut into 8 serving pieces

2   tablespoons butter

12   pearl onions, peeled

5   garlic cloves, minced

¼   cup apple brandy or ¼ cup apple juice

1   cup dry white wine

2   Granny Smith apples, peeled and chopped

8   ounces small button mushrooms

2   teaspoons fresh thyme, chopped

Chicken in white wine is a beloved French dish—and for good reason. It is always delicious. Serve it for a special Sunday dinner or a cozy evening with friends. End the meal the way the French do—with a bakery apple tart. Top each serving with a small scoop of rich vanilla ice cream, and you'll think you're in Paris.

LET'S BEGIN Preheat the oven to 350°F. Combine the flour, salt, and pepper in a shallow dish and dredge the chicken in the mixture. Heat the butter in a large nonstick skillet over medium-high. Add the chicken and cook for 6 minutes, turning once, until browned on both sides. Transfer the chicken to a large casserole dish.

FLASH INTO THE PAN Add the onions and garlic to the skillet, reduce the heat to medium-low, and cook for 2 minutes, or until the garlic is fragrant. Add the apple brandy and white wine and stir to scrape any browned bits off the bottom of the pan.

INTO THE OVEN Transfer the garlic and onion mixture to the casserole with the chicken, then add the apples, mushrooms, and thyme. Cover and bake for 45 minutes, or until chicken is cooked through.

Makes 6 servings

Per serving: 440 calories, 26g protein, 21g carbohydrates, 23g fat, 7g saturated fat, 101mg cholesterol, 313mg sodium

ASIAN BEEF & NOODLES
Prep **10 MINUTES**   *Cook* **12 MINUTES**

1¼   pounds 85% lean ground beef

2   packages (3 ounces each) Oriental-flavored instant ramen noodles, noodles coarsely broken

2   cups frozen broccoli, carrot, red pepper, and water chestnut vegetable blend

2   cups water

¼   teaspoon ground ginger

2   tablespoons thinly sliced scallions

Ramen noodle soup mix gives this dish great flavor, and frozen mixed vegetables cut down on your kitchen time.

LET'S BEGIN Cook the beef in a large nonstick skillet over medium heat for 8 to 10 minutes or until no longer pink, breaking it up with a spoon. Transfer to a bowl using a slotted spoon, then stir in the seasoning packet from one package of the ramen noodles. Pour off any fat from the skillet.

SIMMER & STIR Combine both packets of the noodles, the vegetable blend, water, ginger, and the remaining seasoning packet in the skillet and bring to a boil. Reduce the heat, cover and simmer for 3 minutes or until the noodles are tender, stirring occasionally. Return the beef to the skillet and cook 2 minutes, or until heated through. Stir in the scallions.

Makes 4 servings

Per serving: 496 calories, 36g protein, 31g carbohydrates, 25g fat, 10g saturated fat, 98mg cholesterol, 669mg sodium

Cooking Basics

WONDERFUL WAYS WITH ASIAN NOODLES

Asian dishes are renowned for their an intriguing variety of noodles. Here are the most popular ones you will might try.

FRESH CHINESE EGG NOODLES

Both thin and thick egg noodles are found in Asian markets. They are often neon yellow in color. If you can't find them, fresh or dried Italian pasta makes a good substitute.

RICE NOODLES

Rice noodles come in different thicknesses, both thin (often labeled vermicelli) and wide (also called sticks). Rice noodles are softened in hot water rather than cooked.

CELLOPHANE NOODLES

These noodles have very little taste but happily sop up all the flavors of the dish. Cellophane noodles are prized for their translucency and texture.

UDON NOODLES

Fat, slippery, and white, udon noodles are perfect for robust soups and casseroles. They are often used interchangeably with soba noodles.

SOBA NOODLES

These are Japanese brownish buckwheat noodles that have a tempting nutty flavor and delicate texture. They are typically served cold with a dipping sauce as well as in salads.

SuperQuick

ISLAND CHICKEN STIR-FRY

Prep **10 MINUTES**   *Cook* **13 MINUTES**

Flattening chicken breasts cuts down on the cooking time here and ensures the chicken will cook evenly as well. Serve with steamed white rice and end the meal with fresh fruit sorbet and cookies.

2	boneless, skinless chicken breast halves
⅛	teaspoon ground cinnamon
¼	teaspoon dried oregano leaves, crushed
1	tablespoon olive oil
¾	cup pineapple juice
1	tablespoon lime juice
1	teaspoon cornstarch
1	teaspoon chopped fresh parsley or cilantro

LET'S BEGIN Place the chicken between 2 sheets of plastic wrap and flatten to ½ inch thick using a meat mallet or rolling pin. Sprinkle evenly on both sides with the cinnamon and oregano.

FLASH INTO THE PAN Heat the oil in a medium skillet over medium heat. Cook the chicken for 10 minutes, turning once, until cooked through. Transfer to a serving platter and cover to keep warm. Meanwhile, combine the pineapple juice, lime juice, and cornstarch in a small bowl, stir until well mixed, and set aside.

MAKE IT SAUCY Pour the pineapple juice mixture into the skillet and cook for 1 to 2 minutes, stirring constantly, until the sauce boils and thickens. Stir in the parsley and spoon the sauce over the chicken.

Makes 2 servings

Per serving: 380 calories, 55g protein, 15g carbohydrates, 10g fat, 2g saturated fat, 137mg cholesterol, 155mg sodium

ALASKA SALMON TERIYAKI
Prep **5 MINUTES**   *Cook* **20 MINUTES**

1   cup instant or quick-
     cooking rice

1   can (14¾-ounces)
     Alaska salmon

1   tablespoon vegetable oil

1   package (16 ounces)
     frozen stir-fry vegetable
     blend

½   cup teriyaki marinade
     and sauce

¼   teaspoon dark sesame oil
     (optional)

¼   teaspoon ground ginger
     (optional)

Salmon and teriyaki sauce are a match made in heaven. Though the dark sesame oil and ground ginger are optional, we think they add something special. So add them if they're on hand.

LET'S BEGIN Prepare the rice according to package directions and keep warm. Drain the salmon and reserve 2 tablespoons of liquid from the can. Break the salmon into chunks and set aside.

STIR-FRY Meanwhile, heat the oil in a wok or a large skillet over medium-high heat. Add the vegetables and stir-fry for 1 minute. Stir in the salmon liquid and the teriyaki sauce. Add the sesame oil and ginger, if you wish. Gently stir in the salmon, reduce the heat to medium, cover, and cook for 4 to 5 minutes, or until the vegetables are crisp-tender. Serve the salmon and vegetables over the rice.

Makes 3 servings

Per serving: 436 calories, 34g protein, 39g carbohydrates, 13g fat, 3g saturated fat, 77mg cholesterol, 2,426mg sodium

Time Savers

4 SUPER SHORTCUT SAUCES

Make a sauce fast and easy by starting with a jar.

• Sauté some sliced mushrooms, sliced onion, and small broccoli florets until tender. Pour in a jar of Alfredo sauce and cook until nice and bubbly. Spoon over hot pasta. Sprinkle with crisp crumbled bacon. Dinner!

• Put jarred marinara sauce into a pot along with a drained jar of sliced mushrooms, a small can of sliced ripe olives, and some capers. Let it simmer for about 5 minutes and spoon over grilled or broiled chicken breasts.

• Pour a jar of any favorite salsa into a bowl. Add diced avocado, sliced ripe black olives, thinly sliced celery, and chopped fresh cilantro. Stir it all up and spoon over fish.

• Empty a jar of pesto into a saucepan. Stir in enough heavy cream to make it good and saucy. Let it simmer until bubbly, then remove from the heat and add a handful of freshly grated Parmesan and grated lemon zest. Spoon over steamed green beans, asparagus, or zucchini.

SALSA CHICKEN OLÉ

Prep **5 MINUTES**   *Cook* **15 MINUTES**

1   **pound boneless, skinless chicken breasts, cut into strips**

1   **package (1¼ ounces) taco seasoning**

2   **tablespoons vegetable oil**

1   **can (14½ ounces) diced tomatoes**

⅓   **cup apricot or peach preserves**

Here's a south-of-the-border quick fix we know you'll just love. Apricot preserves contribute just the right amount of sweet-tart flavor, and taco seasoning brings in just enough heat. Serve this dish with warmed-up flour tortillas and lots of chunky guacamole. Yum!

LET'S BEGIN Place the chicken and taco seasoning in a resealable plastic bag, seal, and turn to coat.

FLASH INTO THE PAN Heat the oil in a large skillet over medium heat. Add the chicken, and cook for 5 to 7 minutes, stirring often until lightly browned. Stir in the tomatoes and the preserves, reduce the heat, cover, and simmer for 10 minutes.

Makes 4 servings

Per serving: 309 calories, 29g protein, 25g carbohydrates, 9g fat, 1g saturated fat, 68mg cholesterol, 1,063mg sodium

MEXICAN BEAN & TURKEY BURRITOS

Prep **10 MINUTES**   *Cook* **7 MINUTES**

4	large flour tortillas
¼	cup barbecue sauce
4	ounces thinly sliced deli turkey
4	slices pepper Monterey Jack or American cheese
½	cup black beans, drained, rinsed
½	cup sliced green onions
2	tablespoons butter

Burritos are true comfort food, Tex-Mex-style! Enjoy them.

LET'S BEGIN Spread each tortilla with 1 tablespoon barbecue sauce. In a strip down the center of each tortilla, place one-quarter of the turkey, 1 slice cheese, 2 tablespoons beans, and 2 tablespoons green onion. Fold the top and bottom over, then roll up.

INTO THE PAN Heat the butter in a large skillet over medium heat until sizzling. Add the burritos and cook, turning once, for 5 to 6 minutes, or until brown and heated through.

Makes 4 servings

Per serving: 460 calories, 19g protein, 54g carbohydrates, 16g fat, 10g saturated fat, 45mg cholesterol, 1,370mg sodium

Cooking Basics

MANY WAYS TO FOLD A TORTILLA

In Mexico, the tortilla is the everyday bread. It's round and flat, unleavened, and made from corn or wheat flour. The name comes from the Spanish word *torta*, meaning round cake. Tortillas show up in many dishes:

BURRITOS. Fill flour tortillas with such fillings as shredded cooked beef, refried beans, grated cheese, sour cream, and shredded lettuce. Then fold up opposite ends, enclosing fillings completely inside.

CHIMICHANGAS. Use the large flour tortillas and fill them as you like with ground beef, grated American cheese, refried beans.

Roll them up, tuck in their ends, then fry them until crispy and golden. Top with chunky salsa. guacamole, sour cream, and shredded cheese.

ENCHILADAS. Dip corn tortillas in a red sauce to soften them, fill with cheese, beef, and a few minced chile peppers, if you like. Roll up, sprinkle with cheese, top with salsa, and bake until bubbly.

FAJITAS. Marinate strips of skirt steak in a peppered lime juice and oil mixture overnight, then grill them. Place them in the center of large flour tortillas with condiments such as grilled onions and sweet

peppers, and fold up burrito-style. Serve with salsa and guacamole.

QUESADILLAS. These resemble a large tortilla half-moon-shaped sandwich made from large round flour tortillas. Fill as you like with grated cheese, cooked beef or chicken, and refried beans. Then fold and toast under the broiler until the cheese melts.

TACOS. Fry cornmeal tortillas into crisp half-moon folded pockets. Fill with a variety of fillings: chili-seasoned beef, refried beans, fresh tomatoes, shredded lettuce, chopped onion, grated Cheddar, guacamole, and salsa.

CHICKEN & BLACK BEAN ENCHILADAS

Prep **30 MINUTES**   *Bake* **25 MINUTES**

2   jars (16 ounces each) mild picante sauce

¼   cup chopped fresh cilantro

2   tablespoons chili powder

1   teaspoon ground cumin

2   cups chopped cooked chicken (10 ounces)

1   can (15 ounces) black beans, drained, rinsed

1⅓   cups french-fried onions

10   (7-inch) flour tortillas

1   cup shredded pepper Jack cheese

A cup of pepper Jack cheese adds a healthy amount of bite to these easy enchiladas. If you prefer lots of heat, use hot, rather than mild, picante sauce. And keep the fat calories down by using nonfat flour tortillas, found right next to the regular ones at your grocer's.

LET'S BEGIN Preheat the oven to 350°F. Grease a 15 × 10-inch jelly-roll pan. Combine the picante sauce, cilantro, chili powder, and cumin in a large saucepan. Bring to a boil, then reduce the heat and simmer for 5 minutes.

ROLL 'EM UP Combine 1½ cups of the sauce mixture, the chicken, beans, and ⅔ cup of the onions in a medium bowl. Spoon about ½ cup filling on each tortilla and fold in the top, bottom, and sides. Place seam side down in the prepared pan. Spoon the remaining sauce over the top.

INTO THE OVEN Bake, uncovered, for 20 minutes, or until heated through. Sprinkle with the remaining ⅔ cup onions and the cheese. Bake for 5 minutes longer, or until the cheese is melted. Serve hot.

Makes 5 servings

Per serving: 610 calories, 33g protein, 64g carbohydrates, 23g fat, 9g saturated fat, 70mg cholesterol, 2,393mg sodium

SuperQuick

CURRIED CHICKEN & 'TATER STEW

Prep **6 MINUTES**   *Cook* **24 MINUTES**

1	tablespoon vegetable oil
1	medium onion, thinly sliced
1¼	pounds boneless, skinless chicken thighs, trimmed and cubed
2	garlic cloves, minced
2	teaspoons grated fresh ginger
2	teaspoons curry powder
1	package (16 ounces) refrigerated diced potatoes
1	can (14 ounces) light coconut milk
1	cup frozen peas
Salt	
2	tablespoons chopped fresh cilantro

Here's a super-satisfying way to enjoy a chicken and potatoes meal without fuss but with lots of great flavor. Already-diced potatoes cut way down on your kitchen time, and boneless, skinless chicken thighs take only minutes to cube so they're ready for the pot.

LET'S BEGIN Heat the oil in a large saucepan over medium-high heat. Add the onion and chicken and cook 5 minutes, or until the onion softens, stirring often. Add the garlic, ginger, and curry powder and cook 1 minute.

SIMMER & STIR Add the potatoes and coconut milk and bring to a boil. Reduce the heat to medium-low, cover, and simmer 15 minutes. Stir in the peas and cook 3 minutes, or until heated through. Add salt to taste and stir in the cilantro just before serving.

Makes 4 servings

Per serving: 369 calories, 34g protein, 28g carbohydrates, 15g fat, 10g saturated fat, 118mg cholesterol, 571mg sodium

QUICK PORK FAJITAS

Prep **10 MINUTES**　*Cook* **8 MINUTES**

1　pound pork tenderloin, thinly sliced

3　tablespoons fajita seasoning

1　small onion, sliced

1　small green bell pepper, sliced

4　(8-inch) flour tortillas, warmed

Salsa

Cook the pork and vegetables and heat up the tortillas all on the grill—no pot to clean.

LET'S BEGIN Combine the pork and the seasoning in a medium bowl and toss to coat.

STIR-FRY Heat a large nonstick skillet over medium-high and stir-fry the pork, onion, and pepper for 8 minutes, or until the pork is done and the vegetables are crisp-tender. Wrap the pork and vegetables in the tortillas and serve with salsa.

Makes 4 servings

Per serving: 300 calories, 28g protein, 31g carbohydrates, 7g fat, 2g saturated fat, 75mg cholesterol, 760mg sodium

BEEF STEAK GYROS

Prep **15 MINUTES**　*Cook* **13 MINUTES**

1　teaspoon dried oregano leaves, crushed

1　teaspoon minced garlic

1　pound beef shoulder top blade (flat iron) steaks

Salt and ground black pepper

4　pita rounds, warmed

Tomato slices

Sweet onion slices

Yogurt Sauce (see recipe)

Gyros, a popular Middle Eastern street food, are just as tasty with hot sliced steak as with room temperature steak; the choice is yours.

LET'S BEGIN Heat a large nonstick skillet over medium heat until hot. Press the oregano and garlic evenly onto both sides of the steaks. Cook the steaks for 13 to 15 minutes for medium-rare to medium doneness, turning twice.

STUFF & SERVE Cut the steaks into thin slices and season to taste with salt and pepper. Serve the steak in the pita pockets topped with the tomato and onion slices and the Yogurt Sauce.

YOGURT SAUCE

Stir together 1 cup plain low-fat yogurt, ¼ cup diced cucumber, 1 minced garlic clove, ½ teaspoon salt, and ¼ teaspoon ground black pepper in a small bowl; cover and refrigerate.

Makes 4 servings

Per serving: 410 calories, 34g protein, 41g carbohydrates, 11g fat, 4g saturated fat, 50mg cholesterol, 795mg sodium

Beef Steak Gyros

SuperQuick
CAJUN PORK PAELLA

Prep **10 MINUTES**   *Cook* **15 MINUTES**

There are probably as many versions of this traditional dish as there are Spanish cooks. Cajun seasoning and Cajun-style beans and rice mix bring all the fabulous flavor the dish needs without a lot of measuring.

1   pound boneless pork loin, cut into ½-inch cubes

1   tablespoon Cajun seasoning

1   tablespoon vegetable oil

1   package (7.4 ounces) quick-cooking spicy Cajun-style beans and rice mix

1¼   cups water

¼   cup dry white wine or chicken broth

1   bottle (8 ounces) clam juice or chicken broth

1   jar (6½ ounces) marinated artichoke hearts, drained

1   cup frozen peas, thawed

1   jar (2 ounces) diced pimientos

LET'S BEGIN Combine the pork and the seasoning in a medium bowl and toss to coat. Heat the oil in a large nonstick skillet over medium-high. Brown the pork and cook for 5 minutes, stirring often. Remove from the skillet and keep warm.

SIMMER & STIR Add the beans and rice mix with the seasoning packets to the skillet. Stir in the next 3 ingredients and bring to a boil. Reduce the heat, cover, and simmer for 6 minutes, stirring occasionally. Place the pork and the remaining ingredients on top of the rice mixture, cover, and cook for 4 minutes, or until most of the liquid is absorbed.

Makes 4 servings

Per serving: 450 calories, 36g protein, 48g carbohydrates, 11g fat, 2g saturated fat, 63mg cholesterol, 1,250mg sodium

---

On the Menu

Come on down to Cajun country, where the living is easy, the entertaining welcoming, and the food is bursting with goodness and flavor.

Stuffed Mussels

Gazpacho with Scallion-Red Pepper Garnish

Cajun Pork Paella

Cinnamon Rice Pudding

White Wine Sangria

BOMBAY SHRIMP

Prep **20 MINUTES + MARINATING**   *Cook* **10 MINUTES**

Serve this company-pleaser with an Indian bread, such as nan or poori, sautéed green beans, and lots of cooling fruit sorbet for dessert.

¼ cup olive oil

¼ cup lime juice

¼ cup Calcutta curry seasoning

2 pounds jumbo shrimp, peeled and deveined, tails left on

4 tablespoons butter or margarine

3 tablespoons seeded and minced jalapeño chile peppers

1 cup thinly sliced onion

1 mango, peeled and diced

½ cup sliced scallions

½ teaspoon garlic powder

½ teaspoon ground ginger

¼ cup chicken broth

¼ cup coconut milk

4½ cup hot cooked basmati rice

LET'S BEGIN Stir first 3 ingredients in a large shallow dish. Add shrimp. Toss to coat. Cover and chill for 20 minutes.

INTO THE PAN Remove the shrimp from the marinade (discard marinade). Heat the butter in a large skillet or wok over medium-high heat. Add the shrimp and jalapeño and sauté 3 to 4 minutes, or until shrimp begin to turn opaque. Add the next 5 ingredients and sauté 3 minutes longer. Add broth and milk, bring to a boil, and cook 2 minutes. Serve over rice.

Makes 6 servings

Per serving (includes ¾ cup cooked basmati rice): 500 calories, 28g protein, 51g carbohydrates, 21g fat, 9g saturated fat, 235mg cholesterol, 1,147mg sodium

---

On the Menu

◆

Come along to Bombay, where the cooking is spicy, the flavors are bold, and the sauces are cooling.

◆

Chunky Tomato-Parsley Salad

Lemon-Chili Vinaigrette

Bombay Shrimp

Basmati Rice with Toasted Almonds and Raisins

Cucumber Raita

Mango Chutney

Sliced Oranges Sprinkled with Rose Water

Minted Iced Tea

LOW COUNTRY BOIL
Prep **10 MINUTES**   *Cook* **20 MINUTES**

2 bags (3 ounces each) crab boil mix

2 pounds small whole red potatoes

4 ears corn, each cut in half

1 pound smoked sausage, cut into 3-inch pieces

1 pound medium shrimp

1 pound crawfish

Serve this up just like they do along the banks of the bayou in the low country of Louisiana. Cover your picnic table with newspaper and put out stacks of napkins and a pitcher of iced tea. Y'all come!

LET'S BEGIN Place the crab boil mix in a very large pot, fill half full with water, and bring to a boil.

BOIL & SERVE Add the potatoes and cook for 6 minutes. Add the corn and cook 3 minutes. Add the sausage and cook 3 minutes, then add the shrimp and crawfish and cook 3 minutes longer. Drain and serve immediately.

Makes 8 servings

Per serving: 427 calories, 34g protein, 28g carbohydrates, 20g fat, 7g saturated fat, 152mg cholesterol, 1,028mg sodium

CURRIED PORK SKILLET

Prep **15 MINUTES**   Cook **24 MINUTES**

2   tablespoons Indian Spice Blend (see recipe)

4   boneless pork chops, cut into ¾-inch cubes

1   tablespoon vegetable oil

2   large onions, chopped

3   garlic cloves, crushed

¾   cup beef broth

3   tablespoons honey

2   tablespoons lemon juice

1   cup plain yogurt

2   tablespoons all-purpose flour

¼   cup chopped fresh parsley

3   cups hot cooked white rice

¼   cup chopped cashews

Chopped fresh cilantro

This dish has many spices frequently used in Indian cooking, but don't be discouraged. Mix up a double or triple batch of the spice mix so they are all ready the next time you cook this Indian-inspired skillet dish.

LET'S BEGIN Place the spice mixture in a large resealable plastic bag with the pork and shake to coat. Heat the oil over medium-high heat in a large skillet. Add the onions and garlic and cook, stirring often, for 8 minutes, or until tender. Add the pork and cook, stirring constantly, for 2 to 3 minutes, or until browned.

BUBBLE & STIR Add the broth, honey, and lemon juice and bring to a boil. Reduce the heat, cover, and simmer for 10 minutes, or until the pork is tender.

SAUCE & SERVE Combine the yogurt and flour in a small bowl and stir to mix well. Add the yogurt mixture and the parsley to the skillet and cook for 2 to 3 minutes, stirring constantly, until sauce thickens. Serve over rice and garnish with cashews and cilantro.

INDIAN SPICE BLEND

Combine in a large, resealable plastic bag: 2 teaspoons ground cumin, 1 teaspoon ground cardamom, 1 teaspoon ground cinnamon, 1 teaspoon ground coriander, 1 teaspoon ground mace, ½ teaspoon ground black pepper, and ¼ teaspoon salt. Shake to mix well. **TIP:** *Make double or triple the amount and keep on hand in your spice cabinet.*

Makes 4 servings
Per serving (includes ¾ cup cooked white rice + 1 tablespoon unsalted chopped cashews): 533 calories, 32g protein, 68g carbohydrates, 14g fat, 1g saturated fat, 70mg cholesterol, 252mg sodium

Roast Chicken & Yams, page 133

Dinner with Friends

Remember visiting Grandma every Sunday and sitting down to her delicious pot roast? It was always so tender that you didn't need a knife, and it was so juicy and flavorful that you always had a second helping. Here are many of those down-home comfort foods at their ever-lovin' best. Easy-roast a chicken, bubble up a veal stew, or bake up some mac 'n' cheese. Or some weekend, simmer up a supper of Swiss steak that's so tender it cuts with a fork. These all come with the same homemade taste that many old-fashioned recipes were famous for. But ours have a big difference. They require less time and fuss, thanks to convenience foods and quick-cook techniques. But no one will ever know!

Pot Roast with Vegetables

Prep **10 MINUTES**   *Cook/Bake* **2 HOURS, 5 MINUTES**

1	pound boneless beef top round roast
1	(1 ounce) envelope dry onion soup mix
1	cup water
3	medium potatoes, peeled and quartered
1	package (16 ounces) frozen broccoli, cauliflower, and carrots

Pot roast tops the list of the most popular comfort foods. Dry onion soup mix has all the flavor you need to make a very tasty pot roast. We've used round steak, a cut of meat that loves long cooking.

LET'S BEGIN Preheat the oven to 325°F. Heat a large ovenproof pot over medium-high heat until hot and coat with cooking spray. Cook the roast 5 minutes, turning once, until browned on both sides.

INTO THE OVEN Sprinkle the soup mix evenly on both sides of the roast, add the water, cover, and bake for 1 hour. Add the potatoes, cover, and bake for 30 minutes longer. Stir in the frozen vegetables and bake an additional 30 minutes, or until the vegetables are tender.

Makes 6 servings

Per serving: 300 calories, 30g protein, 27g carbohydrates, 8g fat, 3g saturated fat, 80mg cholesterol, 966mg sodium

Irish Stew

Prep **10 MINUTES**   *Cook* **1¾ HOUR**

1	pound boneless lamb stew meat
4	medium red potatoes
3	carrots
1	onion, sliced
1	teaspoon garlic salt
½	teaspoon garlic powder
½	teaspoon ground black pepper
1¼	cups water
	Chopped fresh parsley (optional)

We love the Irish for their fabulous lamb stew and melt-in-your-mouth scones. If you like, toss in any favorite green vegetable to make this a true one-pot meal.

LET'S BEGIN Peel and cut the potatoes into ½-inch slices. Cut the carrots into ½-inch slices.

BUBBLE & BOIL Combine all the ingredients in a large pot, cover, and bring to a boil over medium-high heat.

SIMMER LOW Reduce heat to medium-low and simmer 1½ hours, or until lamb is tender. Sprinkle each serving with parsley, if you like.

Makes 4 servings

Per serving: 352 calories, 32g protein, 38g carbohydrates, 7g fat, 3g saturated fat, 92mg cholesterol, 675mg sodium

Yellow Tomato Gazpacho

Prep **20 MINUTES + CHILLING**

2½ pounds yellow tomatoes

2 bell peppers (1 yellow, 1 red)

1 cucumber, peeled

¼ cup chopped red onion

¼ cup chopped fresh basil

3 garlic cloves, minced

3 cups tomato juice

1 can (14½ ounces) chicken broth

¼ cup lemon juice

¼ cup honey

¼ cup red wine vinegar

2 tablespoons Worcestershire sauce

Salt and ground black pepper (optional)

Yellow tomatoes have less acidity than red tomatoes. Use your food processor to chop the bell peppers, cucumber, red onion, and garlic—but chop them one at a time to get their texture just right.

LET'S BEGIN Seed and chop the tomatoes, bell peppers, and cucumbers.

FIX IT FAST Combine all the ingredients in a large bowl. Season to taste with salt and pepper, if you like. Cover and refrigerate at least 1 hour or overnight.

Makes 6 servings

Per serving: 130 calories, 5g protein, 30g carbohydrates, 1g fat, 0g saturated fat, 0mg cholesterol, 734mg sodium

Cooking Basics

TOMATOES—PEEL THEM RIGHT

There are lots of recipes that call for removing the flavorless peel from tomatoes because of its texture.

First, to remove the core of the tomato, take a small paring knife and cut around the stem end to remove a cone-shaped plug.

Turn the tomato over, and with the tip of the knife cut an X in the center, being careful not to cut the flesh.

Gently lower the tomato into a pot of boiling water and cook for about 20 seconds. Then with a slotted spoon, quickly remove the tomato and place it in a large bowl of ice water for about 20 seconds to stop the cooking.

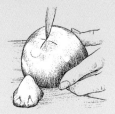

Gently peel away the skin, starting at the X and working your way toward the stem.

JAMBALAYA ON-THE-BAYOU

Prep **15 MINUTES**   *Cook* **35 MINUTES**

2   tablespoons vegetable oil

1   tablespoon all-purpose flour

1   large onion, chopped

½   pound ham, cubed

1   bay leaf, finely crumbled

1   pound medium cooked shrimp

2   large tomatoes, peeled and chopped

¼   cup diced green bell pepper

2   garlic cloves, crushed

1   tablespoon dried parsley flakes

1   teaspoon Creole seasoning

1   cup long-grain parboiled rice (uncooked)

Ground black pepper

Jambalaya is one of the hallmarks of Creole cuisine. Its name is derived from the word jambon *for "ham," which is the main ingredient in many renditions. Our version contains shrimp, but other authentic recipes contain combinations of chicken, pork, and andouille sausage as well.*

LET'S BEGIN Heat the oil in a large pot over medium heat, add the flour, and cook for 5 minutes, stirring constantly, until mixture turns light brown.

BUBBLE & BOIL Stir in the onion, ham, and bay leaf and cook 5 minutes, or until onion softens. Add all the remaining ingredients, except the rice and black pepper and bring to a boil.

SIMMER LOW Stir in the rice, reduce heat, cover, and simmer for 25 minutes or until liquid is absorbed and rice is tender. Season jambalaya to taste with black pepper.

Makes 4 servings
Per serving: 500 calories, 40g protein, 49g carbohydrates, 14g fat, 3g saturated fat, 206mg cholesterol, 1,027mg sodium

---

Food Facts

JAMBALAYA: A MELTING POT!

Jambalaya truly represents what Creole cooking and the various ethnicities found in Louisiana.

The word *jambalaya* comes from the French word *jambon* (for "ham"), the African word *ya* (for "rice"), and the influence of the Acadian language, where things are described as being *a la.*

There are stories on how this dish got its name. One refers to a gentleman visiting New Orleans late one evening. It was well after the dinner hour, and there was little left to eat. The owner asked his cook, Jean, to *balayez*—which, in Acadian, means to mix some things together. The guest was

delighted with the cook's creation and immediately named it Jean Balayez, now known as Jambalaya.

Jambalaya is a versatile and flexible dish, containing many ingredients like rice, tomatoes, onion, green peppers, and meat, fish, or poultry. Jambalaya is truly comfort food—Creole style.

HEARTY ROUND STEAK

Prep **10 MINUTES + MARINATING** *Bake* **1 HOUR**

1	pound round steak, ½-inch thick, well trimmed
¼	cup thick steak sauce
¼	cup fat-free Italian dressing
½	cup chopped onion
2	small garlic cloves, minced
1	pound new potatoes, quartered
8	ounces sliced mushrooms
1	package (16 ounces) frozen mixed broccoli, cauliflower, and carrots

Steak, potatoes, and mushrooms are a combination made in heaven. Use any of your favorite mushrooms here: white, cremini, and portobello will all be delicious. Frozen vegetables eliminate lots of prep, but still add great garden-vegetable flavor to the finished dish.

LET'S BEGIN Spray a large baking dish with cooking spray. Cut the steak into 6 equal portions and place in a single layer in the dish. Mix the steak sauce, dressing, onion, and garlic and pour over the steak. Marinate in the refrigerator for 1 hour.

INTO THE OVEN Preheat the oven to 350°F. Tuck the potatoes and mushrooms around the meat in the dish. Cover with foil. Bake for 45 minutes, or until the potatoes are tender. Add the frozen vegetables, cover, and bake for 15 minutes longer.

Makes 6 servings

Per serving: 190 calories, 18g protein, 25g carbohydrates, 3g fat, 1g saturated fat, 35mg cholesterol, 390mg sodium

SWISS STEAK

Prep **20 MINUTES**   *Cook* **1¾ HOURS**

1½   pounds boneless beef round or chuck shoulder steaks, ½ inch thick

3   tablespoons all-purpose flour

1   teaspoon salt

½   teaspoon ground black pepper

2   tablespoons vegetable oil

¾   cup diced carrots

¾   cup diced onion

¾   cup water

½   cup diced green bell pepper

½   cup diced celery

½   cup picante sauce

¼   cup ketchup

1   tablespoon white vinegar

2½   cups farfalle (bow ties)

Swiss steak is steak that has been pounded to make it as tender as possible. We love round steak and chuck steak because they are both easy on the wallet and very tasty. The bold, simmering sauce of picante, ketchup, and vinegar gives the dish all the great home-cooked flavor, without much work from you.

LET'S BEGIN Cut the steak into 6 equal-sized pieces. Place between 2 layers of plastic wrap and pound to ¼ inch thick. Combine the flour, salt, and pepper in a shallow dish and stir to mix well. Lightly coat the beef with the flour mixture.

BROWN IT Heat half of the oil in a Dutch oven over medium heat until hot. Add half of the beef and cook 4 minutes, until browned, turning once. Remove beef from the pot and repeat with the remaining oil and beef. Pour off the drippings.

SIMMER LOW Return the beef to the Dutch oven and add all the remaining ingredients, except the pasta. Bring to a boil, reduce heat, cover, and simmer 1½ hours, or until the beef is fork-tender, stirring occasionally. If the sauce becomes too thick, stir in a little water.

SERVE IT UP Meanwhile, about 15 minutes before serving, prepare the pasta according to package directions. Drain and keep warm. Serve the beef over the pasta.

Makes 6 servings
Per serving: 380 calories, 27g protein, 25g carbohydrates, 19g fat, 6g saturated fat, 68mg cholesterol, 744mg sodium

SAVORY VEAL STEW

Prep **20 MINUTES**   *Cook* **1 ½ HOURS**

⅓ cup all-purpose flour

½ teaspoon salt

½ teaspoon ground black pepper

2½ pounds boneless veal stew meat, cut into 1-inch pieces

3 tablespoons olive oil

1 large onion, coarsely chopped

3 garlic cloves, minced

1 can (13¾ to 14½ ounces) chicken broth

2 teaspoons dried thyme

1 pound baby carrots

1 pound small red potatoes, halved

1 cup frozen peas

It's hard not to love veal stew. The meat can be counted on to be melt-in-your-mouth tender and is a good partner for all kinds of other ingredients. Here, baby carrots, peas, and red potatoes turn this into the perfect springtime stew.

LET'S BEGIN Combine the flour, salt, and pepper in a shallow dish and stir to mix well. Lightly coat the veal with the flour mixture. Heat half of the oil in a Dutch oven over medium heat until hot. Add half of the veal and cook 3 to 4 minutes, or until lightly browned, stirring often. Remove veal from the pot and repeat with the remaining oil and veal.

SIMMER LOW Add the onion and garlic to the Dutch oven and cook 1 minute, stirring constantly. Add the veal, broth, and thyme and bring to a boil. Reduce the heat, cover, and simmer 45 minutes.

BUBBLE & STIR Add the carrots and potatoes and stir to combine. Cover and cook 30 minutes, or until veal and vegetables are fork-tender. Then skim any fat from the surface of the stew. Stir in the peas and cook 3 minutes, or until heated through.

Makes 6 servings

Per serving: 420 calories, 43g protein, 31g carbohydrates, 12g fat, 2g saturated fat, 159mg cholesterol, 703mg sodium

POTATO BACON CASSEROLE

Prep **10 MINUTES**   *Bake* **1 HOUR + STANDING**

4   cups frozen shredded hash brown potatoes

½   cup finely chopped onion

8   ounces bacon or turkey bacon, cooked and crumbled

4   ounces shredded Cheddar cheese (1 cup)

1   can (12 ounces) evaporated milk

1   large egg

1½   teaspoons seasoned salt

Casseroles say home cooking, and this one is no exception. Bacon, hash brown potatoes, and chopped onion add up to the best kind of diner comfort food. Preshredded cheese and frozen hash browns make it fast, easy, and delicious.

LET'S BEGIN Preheat the oven to 350°F. Coat an 8-inch-square baking dish with cooking spray.

LAYER Stack up half of the potatoes, onion, bacon, and cheese in the baking dish. Repeat the layering with the remaining half. Whisk together the milk, egg, and seasoned salt in a small bowl and pour evenly over the potato mixture.

INTO THE OVEN Cover with foil and bake for 55 to 60 minutes. Uncover and bake for 5 minutes longer. Let stand for 10 minutes for easier serving.

Makes 4 servings

Per serving: 902 calories, 41g protein, 56g carbohydrates, 59g fat, 25g saturated fat, 170mg cholesterol, 2,217mg sodium

COUNTRY CHICKEN & VEGETABLES

Prep **10 MINUTES**   *Cook* **8 HOURS**

This is food cooked the old-fashioned way: long and slow. Packaged gravy mix and poultry seasoning makes this one-pot dish ever so tasty without fuss. Baby-cut carrots are fun to eat and just the perfect size, but if you like, peel and coarsely chop regular carrots.

1½   pounds potatoes, peeled and cut into 1-inch pieces

½   pound baby carrots

1   medium onion, coarsely chopped

4   bone-in chicken breasts (about 2¼ pounds)

2   (0.87 ounce) packages chicken gravy mix

1   teaspoon dried thyme

¼   teaspoon poultry seasoning or ground sage

1   teaspoon seasoned salt

1½   cups water

1   cup sour cream

LET'S BEGIN Place the potatoes, carrots, and onion in a 3½- or 4-quart slow cooker. Cut each chicken breast in half crosswise and place on top of the vegetables.

SIMMER LOW Combine the next 5 ingredients in a small bowl, stir to mix well, and pour over the chicken. Cover and cook on Low for 8 hours, or until the chicken is cooked through and the vegetables are tender.

MAKE IT SAUCY Remove the chicken and vegetables to a serving platter. Whisk the sour cream into the drippings in the slow cooker and ladle over the chicken and vegetables.

Makes 6 servings

Per serving: 362 calories, 40g protein, 28g carbohydrates, 10g fat, 4g saturated fat, 101mg cholesterol, 806mg sodium

Cooking Basics

ADAPTING A RECIPE TO A SLOW COOKER

Choose a favorite recipe that uses a less tender cut of meat, such as beef chuck or pork shoulder—cuts that love to be slow-cooked. Be sure to trim off any visible fat. Cut up any vegetables into uniform-size pieces and place them in the bottom of the cooker. Set the meat on top of the vegetables.

Since liquids don't boil away like they do in a regular pot, reduce the total amount of liquid by half (unless the dish contains rice).

Finally, if your recipe calls for dairy products, such as milk, cream, or cheese, you need to change the method a bit, since these foods tend to break down during long cooking. Stir in milk or cream during the last 30 minutes of cooking and add any cheese just before serving.

Now sit back, relax, and enjoy your slow cooker.

EASY ROAST CHICKEN DINNER

Prep **15 MINUTES**   *Bake* **1¼ HOURS**

1   tablespoon all-purpose flour

1   teaspoon garlic salt

1   large (14 × 20-inch) oven bag

1   medium onion, cut into eight wedges

2   stalks celery, cut in ½-inch slices (optional)

1   pound baby red potatoes

8   ounces baby carrots

1   chicken (4- to 5-pounds) (neck and giblets removed)

1   tablespoon vegetable oil (optional)

1   teaspoon paprika

An old-fashioned roast chicken cooked nice and slow is a treat we all recall from Grandma's day. This recipe has all the great taste we remember, but cooking the chicken in a bag is so much easier. So reminisce to your heart's content.

LET'S BEGIN Preheat the oven to 350°F. Place the flour and ½ teaspoon of the garlic salt in the oven bag and shake to combine. Place the bag in a 13 × 9-inch baking pan.

SEASON & SPICE Place the vegetables in the oven bag and turn the bag to coat with the seasoned flour. Push the vegetables to the outer edges of the bag. Brush the chicken with the oil, if you wish, and rub with the paprika and the remaining ½ teaspoon garlic salt.

INTO THE OVEN Place the chicken in the center of the bag. Close the bag with the nylon tie and cut six ½-inch slits in the top. Bake for 1¼ to 1½ hours, or until chicken is cooked through and vegetables are tender.

Makes 5 servings

Per serving: 490 calories, 44g protein, 26g carbohydrates, 23g fat, 7g saturated fat, 131mg cholesterol, 482mg sodium

ROAST CHICKEN & YAMS

Prep **10 MINUTES**   *Bake* **50 MINUTES**

1	pound sweet potatoes, peeled and thinly sliced
4	bone-in chicken breast halves (about 2¼ pounds)
1	can (16 ounces) whole berry or jellied cranberry sauce
¼	cup olive or vegetable oil
½	teaspoon ground ginger
½	teaspoon salt
¼	teaspoon ground black pepper

If you love Thanksgiving and all of the fixings, this recipe is for you! Save time by using drained canned sweet potatoes. We've left the bone in the chicken—it adds lots of flavor and is less expensive than boneless chicken breasts.

LET'S BEGIN Preheat the oven to 375°F. Place the potatoes in a 13 × 9-inch baking pan, then place the chicken on top. Whisk the remaining ingredients together in a medium bowl and pour over the chicken.

INTO THE OVEN Bake, uncovered, for 50 minutes or until chicken is cooked and the potatoes are tender.

Makes 4 servings

Per serving: 591 calories, 39g protein, 67g carbohydrates, 18g fat, 4g saturated fat, 103mg cholesterol, 445mg sodium

MAC 'N' CHEESE WITH A TWIST

Prep **10 MINUTES**   *Cook/Bake* **40 MINUTES**

1	pound rotini, macaroni, or other medium pasta
2	tablespoons butter or margarine
6	tablespoons all-purpose flour
2	cups milk
6	ounces shredded Cheddar cheese (1½ cups)
¼	teaspoon cayenne pepper
1	teaspoon salt
⅓	cup grated Parmesan cheese

This dish is a keeper—thanks to two kinds of cheese and a touch of cayenne pepper. To reduce your time in the kitchen, use preshredded Cheddar and grated Parmesan cheese.

LET'S BEGIN Preheat the oven to 375°F. Prepare the pasta according to package directions, drain, and set aside.

MAKE IT SAUCY Meanwhile, melt the butter in a large saucepan over medium heat. Whisk in the flour and cook 1 minute, stirring constantly. Gradually whisk in the milk and bring to a boil, stirring constantly until thickened. Remove the pan from the heat and add the Cheddar cheese, cayenne, and salt and whisk until the cheese melts. Add the pasta and stir until well combined.

INTO THE OVEN Spoon the mixture into a 1½-quart casserole, sprinkle with the Parmesan, and bake for 30 to 35 minutes, or until heated through and top is golden brown.

Makes 6 servings

Per serving: 527 calories, 22g protein, 68g carbohydrates, 19g fat, 10g saturated fat, 52mg cholesterol, 700mg sodium

---

Food Facts

MAC 'N' CHEESE HISTORY

Macaroni and cheese, one of the true American classics, has been enjoyed since Thomas Jefferson served macaroni layered with shredded cheese and butter at Monticello, his home in Virginia.

Cookbook author Mary Randolph provided the first written recipe for macaroni and cheese in her book, *The Virginia House-Wife*, in 1824. Other recipes soon appeared, but none included the all-familiar (and beloved) cheese sauce. That didn't happen until 1915 when *The Larkin Housewives' Cook Book* offered a recipe called English Style Macaroni. In the 1940s and 1950s, recipes containing cheese sauce variations began showing up.

In 1937, Kraft introduced the first instant macaroni and cheese dinner. The commercials promised "a meal for four in nine minutes for an everyday price of 19 cents." Eight million Kraft dinners were sold that year. Today hundreds of millions of boxes are sold each year.

BRUNCH SAUSAGE CASSEROLE

Prep **10 MINUTES + CHILLING**   *Cook/Bake* **61 MINUTES + STANDING**

1	pound bulk pork sausage
4	cups day-old white bread cubes
8	ounces shredded sharp Cheddar cheese (2 cups)
2	cans (12 ounces each) evaporated milk
10	large eggs
1	teaspoon mustard powder
¼	teaspoon onion powder

Pork sausage does fabulous things to bread pudding. This is perfect brunch food, especially since it is prepared ahead and refrigerated overnight before being baked. Serve with a sliced tomato salad and end with sour cream coffee cake and lots of fresh berries and coffee.

LET'S BEGIN Cook the sausage in a large skillet over medium heat for 6 minutes, or until browned, breaking it up with a spoon. Drain off the fat. Coat a 13 × 9-inch baking dish with cooking spray. Place the bread in the baking dish and sprinkle with the cheese. Whisk together the last 4 ingredients in a medium bowl until well combined. Pour the mixture over the bread and cheese. Sprinkle with the sausage. Cover and refrigerate overnight.

INTO THE OVEN Preheat the oven to 325°F. Uncover the casserole and bake for 55 to 60 minutes, or until the cheese is golden brown. Cover with foil if the top begins to brown too quickly while baking. Let the casserole stand for 5 minutes for easier serving.

Makes 8 servings
Per serving: 430 calories, 25g protein, 10g carbohydrates, 31g fat, 13g saturated fat, 335mg cholesterol, 743mg sodium

Mom's Macaroni & Cheese

Prep **10 MINUTES**   *Cook/Bake* **32 MINUTES**

1¾   cups uncooked macaroni

3   tablespoons butter or margarine

2   tablespoons all-purpose flour

½   teaspoon salt

2   cups milk

8   ounces shredded sharp Cheddar cheese (2 cups)

Sharp Cheddar cheese gives this dish an extra oomph.

LET'S BEGIN Preheat the oven to 350°F. Prepare the pasta according to package directions, drain, and set aside.

MAKE IT SAUCY Meanwhile, melt the butter in a large saucepan over medium heat. Stir in the flour and salt and cook 2 minutes, stirring constantly. Gradually add the milk, and cook 3 to 5 minutes, or until sauce boils and thickens, stirring constantly. Add 1½ cups of the cheese and cook for 1 to 2 minutes, or until cheese melts, stirring constantly. Remove from the heat, add the pasta, and stir to mix well.

INTO THE OVEN Spoon the mixture into a 1½-quart casserole, sprinkle with the remaining ½ cup cheese, and bake for 20 minutes, or until heated through.

Makes 6 servings

Per serving: 388 calories, 17g protein, 31g carbohydrates, 22g fat, 13g saturated fat, 64mg cholesterol, 509mg sodium

Pork & Wild Rice Bake

Prep **5 MINUTES**   *Bake* **35 MINUTES**

1   package (6 ounces) long-grain and wild rice mix

2   cups water

1⅓   cups french-fried onions

1   package (10 ounces) frozen cut green beans, thawed, drained

¼   cup orange juice

1   teaspoon grated orange zest

4   boneless pork chops (1 inch thick)

This dish couldn't be faster or more delicious! No one will ever know how easy it was to make!

LET'S BEGIN Preheat the oven to 375°F. Combine the rice mix, water, ⅔ cup of the onions, the green beans, orange juice, and orange zest in a shallow 2-quart baking dish. Arrange the pork chops on top.

INTO THE OVEN Bake, uncovered, for 30 minutes, or until the pork chops are no longer pink in the center. Sprinkle with the remaining ⅔ cup onions and bake for 5 minutes longer, or until the onions are golden. Serve hot.

Makes 4 servings

Per serving: 462 calories, 30g protein, 47g carbohydrates, 17g fat, 5g saturated fat, 62mg cholesterol, 817mg sodium

Mom's Macaroni and Cheese

SOUTHWESTERN CORN SOUFFLÉ

Prep **20 MINUTES**   *Bake* **1 HOUR**

Everyone loves to eat a soufflé, but preparing one can be a little daunting. Here we take all of the worry out of preparing it, and this one is so very tasty. Be sure to beat the egg whites just until stiff peaks form (which you can tell by lifting up the beaters).

3	tablespoons butter or margarine
¼	cup all-purpose flour
1	can (5 ounces) evaporated milk
⅓	cup water
1	can (11 ounces) Mexican-style corn, drained
1	can (4 ounces) chopped green chiles
3	large eggs, separated
3	ounces shredded Cheddar cheese (¾ cup)

LET'S BEGIN Preheat the oven to 325°F. Coat a 1½-quart baking dish with cooking spray. Melt the butter in a large saucepan over medium heat. Add the flour and cook for 1 minute, stirring constantly. Gradually stir in the milk and water and cook, stirring constantly, until the mixture comes to a boil. Remove from the heat and stir in the corn, chiles, egg yolks, and ½ cup of the cheese.

BEAT & FOLD IN Place the egg whites in a medium bowl and beat at high speed with an electric mixer until stiff peaks form. Gently fold the egg whites into the corn mixture and transfer to the baking dish.

INTO THE OVEN Bake for 50 to 55 minutes, or until a knife inserted near the center comes out clean. Top the soufflé with the remaining cheese and bake for 2 to 3 minutes longer, or until the cheese melts.

Makes 6 servings

Per serving: 250 calories, 10g protein, 17g carbohydrates, 16g fat, 8g saturated fat, 144mg cholesterol, 330mg sodium

---

On the Menu

Here's a flavor-packed south-of-the-border menu that will make you think you're in Old Mexico.

Grilled Shrimp with Salsa and Sliced Avocado

Mexican Tortilla Soup

Southwestern Corn Soufflé

Flan

Coffee with Cinnamon

CREDITS

PAGE 2 Cattlemen's Beef Association: Photo for Autumn Beef Stew courtesy of Cattlemen's Beef Board and National Cattlemen's Beef Association. Used with permission.

PAGE 8 Nestlé: Photo for Creamy Tuna Noodle Casserole courtesy of Nestlé. Used with permission.

PAGE 12 National Pork Board: Photo for Cajun Pork Paella courtesy of the National Pork Board. Used with permission.

PAGE 17 Nestlé: Photo for Chicken & Rice Casserole courtesy of Nestlé. Used with permission.

PAGES 18 & 20 Nestlé: Recipe and photo for Chicken & Rice Casserole courtesy of Nestlé. Used with permission.

PAGE 21 Nestlé: Recipe and photo for Creamy Tuna Noodle Casserole courtesy of Nestlé. Used with permission.

PAGE 22 Del Monte Foods: Recipe for Easy Chicken & Rice Bake courtesy of Del Monte Foods. Used with permission.

PAGE 23 Kikkoman: Recipe for Spicy Beef & Biscuits courtesy of Kikkoman. Used with permission.

PAGE 23 Nestlé: Recipe and photo for Cheesy Tuna & Rice courtesy of Nestlé. Used with permission.

PAGES 24/25 Nestlé: Recipe and photo for Cheesy Grits courtesy of Nestlé. Used with permission.

PAGE 26 McCormick: Recipe for Terrific Tuna Tetrazzini courtesy of McCormick. Used with permission.

PAGE 27 Cattlemen's Beef Board: Recipe and photo for Cheese Steak Pizza courtesy of Cattlemen's Beef Board and National Cattlemen's Beef Association. Used with permission.

PAGE 28 Wish-Bone: Recipe for Vegetable-Topped Fish Pouches courtesy of Wish-Bone. Used with permission.

PAGE 29 Reynolds: Recipe for Savory Salmon Provençal courtesy of Reynolds Kitchens. Used with permission.

PAGES 30/31 Cattlemen's Beef Board: Recipe and photo for Easy Beef Potpie courtesy of Cattlemen's Beef Board and National Cattlemen's Beef Association. Used with permission.

PAGE 32 Cattlemen's Beef Board: Photo for Easy Beef Potpie courtesy of Cattlemen's Beef Board and National Cattlemen's Beef Association. Used with permission.

PAGE 34 Birds Eye Foods: Recipe for Sweet & Sour Pork courtesy of Birds Eye Foods. Used with permission.

PAGE 34 United States Potato Board: Recipe for Pork & Potatoes Provençal courtesy of the United States Potato Board. Used with permission.

PAGE 35 Uncle Ben's: Recipe for Stir-Fried Chicken & Rice courtesy of UNCLE BEN's® Brand. Used with permission.

PAGE 36 Cattlemen's Beef Board: Recipe for Beefy Vegetable Skillet courtesy of Cattlemen's Beef Board and National Cattlemen's Beef Association. Used with permission.

PAGE 37 Del Monte Foods: Recipe for Snappin' Beef 'n' Rice courtesy of Del Monte Foods. Used with permission.

PAGE 38 Zatarain's: Recipe for Beefy Red Beans & Rice courtesy of Zatarain's. Used with permission.

PAGE 39 McCormick: Recipe and photo for Super Skillet Mac courtesy of McCormick. Used with permisison

PAGE 40 Del Monte Foods: Recipe for Creamy Skillet Turkey courtesy of Del Monte Foods. Used with permission.

PAGE 41 Birds Eye Foods: Recipe for Turkey Dijon courtesy of Birds Eye Foods. Used with permission.

PAGE 41 Del Monte Foods: Recipe for Hearty Chicken Stew courtesy of Del Monte Foods. Used with permission.

PAGES 42/43 McCormick: Recipe and photo for E-Z Street Gumbo courtesy of McCormick. Used with permission.

PAGE 44 National Pork Board: Recipe and photo for Country Pork Skillet courtesy of National Pork Board. Used with permission.

PAGE 45 McCormick: Recipe for Fat Tuesday Noodles courtesy of McCormick. Used with permission.

PAGE 46 McCormick: Recipe for Chesapeake Bay Pasta courtesy of McCormick. Used with permission.

PAGE 47 National Honey Board: Recipe and photo for Linguini with Honey-Sauced Prawns courtesy of the National Honey Board. Used with permission.

PAGE 48 Uncle Ben's: Recipe for Lemon Shrimp Rice courtesy of UNCLE BEN'S® Brand. Used with permission.

PAGE 49 National Pasta Association: Recipe for Zippy Ziti courtesy of the National Pasta Association. Used with permission.

PAGE 50 National Pork Board: Recipe for Spicy Pork Noodles courtesy of the National Pork Board. Used with permission.

PAGE 51 Del Monte Foods: Recipe for Parmesan Noodle Skillet courtesy of Del Monte Foods. Used with permission.

PAGES 52/53 Catfish Institute: Recipe and photo for Catfish 'n' Pasta courtesy of The Catfish Institute. Used with permission.

PAGE 54 Tone Brothers: Photo for Thai Turkey Sandwiches courtesy of Tone Brothers, Inc., producer of Tone's, Spice Islands, and Durkee products. Used with permission.

PAGE 56 Tone Brothers: Recipe for Curried Chicken Salad courtesy of Tone Brothers, Inc., producer of Tone's, Spice Islands, and Durkee products. Used with permission.

PAGE 57 California Strawberry Commission: Recipe for Strawberry Turkey Salad courtesy of the California Strawberry Commission. Used with permission.

PAGE 58 Kikkoman: Recipe for Southwestern Chicken Salad courtesy of Kikkoman. Used with permission.

PAGE 59 Wish-Bone: Recipe for Gala Salad Toss courtesy of Wish-Bone. Used with permission.

PAGE 60 Association for Dressings & Sauces: Recipe for Caesar Salad courtesy of The Association for Dressings & Sauces. Used with permission.

PAGE 61 Wish-Bone: Recipe for California Cobb Salad courtesy of Wish-Bone. Used with permission.

PAGE 61 Wish-Bone: Recipe for Hearty Summer Salad courtesy of Wish-Bone. Used with permission.

PAGE 62 Kraft Foods: Recipe for Classic Hero courtesy of Kraft Kitchens. Used with permission.

PAGE 63 National Honey Board: Recipe and photo for Honey Couscous Salad courtesy of the National Honey Board. Used with permission.

PAGES 64/65 Association for Dressings & Sauces: Recipe and photo for Ranch-hand Roasted Beef courtesy of The Association for Dressings & Sauces. Used with permission.

PAGE 66 National Pork Board: Recipe and photo for Pork Po' Boys courtesy of the National Pork Board. Used with permission.

PAGE 67 McCormick: Recipe and photo for Sloppy Joe Subs courtesy of McCormick. Used with permission.

PAGE 68 Tone Brothers: Recipe for Green Bean & Potato Parisienne courtesy of Tone Brothers, Inc., producer of Tone's, Spice Islands, and Durkee products. Used with permission.

PAGES 68/69 Cattlemen's Beef Board: Recipe and photo for Speedy Meatball Sandwiches courtesy of Cattlemen's Beef Board and National Cattlemen's Beef Association. Used with permission.

PAGES 70/71 Tone Brothers: Recipe and photo for Thai Turkey Sandwiches courtesy of Tone Brothers, Inc., producer of Tone's, Spice Islands, and Durkee products. Used with permission.

PAGE 72 National Pork Board: Recipe for Pork Pita Pockets courtesy of the National Pork Board. Used with permission.

PAGE 73 McCormick: Recipe and photo for Szechwan Sausage Wraps courtesy of McCormick. Used with permission.

PAGE 74 Cattlemen's Beef Board: Recipe and photo for Mediterranean Steak Sandwiches courtesy of Cattlemen's Beef Board and National Cattlemen's Beef Association. Used with permission.

PAGE 75 National Honey Board: Recipe and photo for Teriyaki Turkey Burgers courtesy of the National Honey Board. Used with permission.

PAGE 76 Association for Dressings & Sauces: Recipe for Southwestern Roll-Ups courtesy of The Association for Dressings & Sauces. Used with permission.

PAGES 76/77 Land O'Lakes: Recipe and photo for Berry Turkey Bagel courtesy of Land O'Lakes, Inc. Used with permission.

PAGE 78 Cattlemen's Beef Board: Photo for Autumn Beef Stew courtesy of Cattlemen's Beef Board and National Cattlemen's Beef Association. Used with permission.

PAGE 80 Land O'Lakes: Recipe and photo for Lemon Dill Salmon with Red Potatoes courtesy of Land O'Lakes, Inc. Used with permission.

PAGE 81 Birds Eye Foods: Recipe for Asparagus, Shrimp & Angel Hair courtesy of Birds Eye Foods. Used with permission.

PAGE 82 Tone Brothers: Recipe for Slow Cookin' Corn Chowder courtesy of Tone Brothers, Inc., producer of Tone's, Spice Islands, and Durkee products. Used with permission.

PAGE 83 Tone Brothers: Recipe for Herb 'Tater Pot courtesy of Tone Brothers, Inc., producer of Tone's, Spice Islands, and Durkee products. Used with permission.

PAGE 84 Del Monte Foods: Recipe for Ham 'n' Cheese Pasta courtesy of Del Monte Foods. Used with permission.

PAGE 85 Birds Eye Foods: Recipe for Western Wagon Wheels courtesy of Birds Eye Foods. Used with permission.

PAGE 85 Kraft Foods: Recipe for Chicken Broccoli Mac courtesy of Kraft Kitchens. Used with permission.

PAGES 86/87 Mrs. T's Pierogies: Recipe and photo for Pierogies Pesto courtesy of Mrs. T's Pierogies. Used with permission.

PAGES 88/89 Cattlemen's Beef Board: Recipe and photo for Autumn Beef Stew courtesy of Cattlemen's Beef Board and National Cattlemen's Beef Association. Used with permission.

PAGE 90 Cattlemen's Beef Board: Recipe for Fast & Easy Beef Chili Pot courtesy of Cattlemen's Beef Board and National Cattlemen's Beef Association. Used with permission.

PAGE 91 Birds Eye Foods: Recipe for Shrimp Creole Stew courtesy of Birds Eye Foods. Used with permission.

PAGES 92/93 Mrs. T's Pierogies: Recipe and photo for Shrimp Gumbo courtesy of Mrs. T's Pierogies. Used with permission.

PAGE 94 French's: Recipe for Zesty Chicken & Vegetable Soup courtesy of Frank's® RedHot® Cayenne Pepper Sauce. Used with permission.

PAGE 95 French's: Recipe for Green Bean & Turkey Bake courtesy of French's® French Fried Onions. Used with permission.

PAGE 96 Cattlemen's Beef Board: Photo for Asian Beef & Noodles courtesy of Cattlemen's Beef Board and National Cattlemen's Beef Association. Used with permission.

PAGE 98 Cattlemen's Beef Board: Recipe and photo for No-Fuss Beef Lasagna courtesy of Cattlemen's Beef Board and National Cattlemen's Beef Association. Used with permission.

PAGE 99 Land O'Lakes: Recipe for Beef & Noodles Stroganoff courtesy of Land O'Lakes, Inc. Used with permission.

WEB SITES

PAGES 100/101 Nestlé: Recipe and photo for Fettucine Primavera courtesy of Nestlé. Used with permission.

PAGE 102 Kikkoman: Recipe for Chicken Lo Mein courtesy of Kikkoman. Used with permission.

PAGE 103 National Chicken Council: Recipe for Coq au Vin Blanc courtesy of the National Chicken Council/U.S. Poultry & Egg Association. Used with permission.

PAGES 104/105 Cattlemen's Beef Board: Recipe and photo for Asian Beef & Noodles courtesy of Cattlemen's Beef Board and National Cattlemen's Beef Association. Used with permission.

PAGE 106 Nestlé: Recipe for Island Chicken Stir-Fry courtesy of Nestlé. Used with permission.

PAGE 107 Nestlé: Recipe for Alaska Salmon Teriyaki courtesy of Nestlé. Used with permission.

PAGE 108 McCormick: Recipe and photo for Salsa Chicken Olé courtesy of McCormick. Used with permission.

PAGE 109 Land O'Lakes: Recipe for Mexican Bean & Turkey Burritos courtesy of Land O'Lakes, Inc. Used with permission.

PAGE 110 French's: Recipe for Chicken & Black Bean Enchiladas courtesy of French's® French Fried Onions. Used with permission.

PAGE 111 United States Potato Board: Recipe and photo for Curried Chicken & 'Tater Stew courtesy of the United States Potato Board. Used with permission.

PAGE 112 National Pork Board: Recipe for Quick Pork Fajitas courtesy of the National Pork Board. Used with permission.

PAGES 112/113 Cattlemen's Beef Board: Recipe and photo for Beef Steak Gyros courtesy of Cattlemen's Beef Board and National Cattlemen's Beef Association. Used with permission.

PAGES 114/115 National Pork Board: Recipe and photo for Cajun Pork Paella courtesy of the National Pork Board. Used with permission.

PAGE 116 Tone Brothers: Recipe for Bombay Shrimp courtesy of Tone Brothers, Inc. producer of Tone's, Spice Islands, and Durkee products. Used with permission.

PAGE 117 Masterbuilt Outdoor Products: Recipe for Low Country Boil courtesy of Masterbuilt Outdoor Products. Used with permission.

PAGES 118/119 National Pork Board: Recipe and photo for Curried Pork Skillet courtesy of the National Pork Board. Used with permission.

PAGE 120 Ocean Spray Cranberries: Photo for Roast Chicken & Yams courtesy of Ocean Spray Cranberries, Inc. Used with permission.

PAGE 122 Birds Eye Foods: Recipe for Pot Roast with Vegetables courtesy of Birds Eye Foods. Used with permission.

PAGE 122 Tone Brothers: Recipe for Irish Stew courtesy of Tone Brothers, Inc. producer of Tone's, Spice Islands, and Durkee products. Used with permission.

PAGE 123 National Honey Board: Recipe for Yellow Tomato Gazpacho courtesy of the National Honey Board. Used with permission.

PAGE 124 Zatarain's: Recipe for Jambalaya on-the-Bayou courtesy of Zatarain's. Used with permission.

PAGE 125 Kraft Foods: Recipe and photo for Hearty Round Steak courtesy of Kraft Kitchens. Used with permission.

PAGES 126/127 Cattlemen's Beef Board: Recipe and photo for Swiss Steak courtesy of Cattlemen's Beef Board and National Cattlemen's Beef Association. Used with permission.

PAGES 128/129 Cattlemen's Beef Board: Recipe and photo for Savory Veal Stew courtesy of Cattlemen's Beef Board and National Cattlemen's Beef Association. Used with permission.

PAGE 130 Nestlé: Recipe and photo for Potato Bacon Casserole courtesy of Nestlé. Used with permission.

PAGE 131 McCormick: Recipe for Country Chicken & Vegetables courtesy of McCormick. Used with permission.

PAGE 132 Reynolds: Recipe for Easy Roast Chicken Dinner courtesy of Reynolds Kitchens. Used with permission.

PAGE 133 Ocean Spray Cranberries: Recipe and photo for Roast Chicken & Yams courtesy of Ocean Spray Cranberries, Inc. Used with permission.

PAGE 134 National Pasta Association: Recipe for Mac 'n' Cheese with a Twist courtesy of the National Pasta Association. Used with permission.

PAGE 135 Nestlé: Recipe and photo for Brunch Sausage Casserole courtesy of Nestlé. Used with permission.

PAGE 136 French's: Recipe for Pork & Wild Rice Bake courtesy of French's® French Fried Onions. Used with permission.

PAGES 136/137 Kraft Foods: Recipe and photo for Mom's Macaroni & Cheese courtesy of Kraft Kitchens. Used with permission.

PAGES 138/139 Nestlé: Recipe and photo for Southwestern Corn Souffle courtesy of Nestlé. Used with permission.

RODALE INC.
www.rodale.com

The Association for Dressings and Sauces
www.dressings-sauces.org

Birds Eye Foods
www.birdseyefoods.com

California Strawberry Commission
www.calstrawberry.com

.
The Catfish Institute
www.catfishinstitute.com

Cattlemen's Beef Board and National Cattlemen's Beef Association
www.beefitswhatsfordinner.com

Del Monte Foods
www.delmonte.com

Frank's® RedHot® Cayenne Pepper Sauce; French's® French Fried Onions
www.frenchsfoods.com

Kikkoman
www.kikkoman.com

Kraft Kitchens
www.kraftfoods.com

Land O'Lakes, Inc.
www.landolakes.com

Masterbuilt Outdoor Products
www.masterbuilt.com

McCormick
www.mccormick.com

Mrs. T's Pierogies
www.pierogies.com

National Chicken Council/U.S. Poultry & Egg Association
www.eatchicken.com

National Honey Board
www.honey.com

National Pasta Association
www.ilovepasta.org

National Pork Board
www.otherwhitemeat.com

Nestlé
www.verybestbaking.com

Ocean Spray Cranberries, Inc.
www.oceanspray.com

Reynolds Kitchens
www.reynoldskitchen.com

Tone Brothers, Inc., producer of Tone's, Spice Islands, and Durkee products
www.spiceadvice.com

UNCLE BEN'S® Brand
www.unclebens.com

United States Potato Board
www.potatohelp.com

Wish-Bone
www.wish-bone.com

Zatarain's
www.zatarain.com

INDEX

✔ Designates a SuperQuick recipe that gets you in and out of the kitchen in 30 minutes or less!
Boldface page numbers refer to photographs. *Italicized* page numbers refer to boxed text.